THERE AND BACK AGAIN:
AN ENGINEER'S TALE

(Miscellaneous Ramblings of an Aerospace Engineer)

THERE AND BACK AGAIN:
AN ENGINEER'S TALE

(Miscellaneous Ramblings of an Aerospace Engineer)

Ron Phillips

This book is dedicated to the aircrew who fly the F-15 Eagle,
for it is their butts in the seats and their lives on the line.

It is the aircrew who must ultimately rely on the engineers who design the
aircraft, rely on the machinists and technicians who build the aircraft,
and rely on the maintainers who keep the aircraft flying.

TABLE OF CONTENTS

Preface ix

Chapter 0 Expectations 1

Chapter 1 Choosing a Career 5

Chapter 2 Off to College 10

Chapter 3 My First Assignment 23

Chapter 4 Engineer Versus Pilot – An Introduction 32

Chapter 5 Test Pilots Versus Mere Mortal Pilots 40

Chapter 6 Not All Test Pilots are the Same 46

Chapter 7 Not All Test Pilots are the Same – Part Deux 51

Chapter 8 Life in the Desert 55

Chapter 9 A Keep Eagle Story 60

Chapter 10 China Lake – a Travel Story 65

Chapter 11 Life in the Desert – Part Deux 70

Chapter 12 Happy Hour 77

Chapter 13 In the Beginning... 83

Chapter 14 Sonic Booms 86

Chapter 15 A Stereotypical Engineer 90

Chapter 16 Proper Use of Technology 94

Chapter 17 Flight Test Equipment? 97

Chapter 18 Fresh 100

Chapter 19 There and Back Again 104

Chapter 20 Life in the Defense/Aerospace Industry 108

Chapter 21 One of the Fun Missions 111

Chapter 22 In Memoriam 113

Chapter 23 End of a Career 118

Chapter 24 Acknowledgements 122

Acronyms / Abbreviations / Definitions 129

PREFACE

Being a semi-retired, semi-unemployed engineer, I find myself a bit long on time and short on cash. Good news. Ex-engineers don't just sit around whining about problems; no, we figure out ways to fix them. We fix things, it's just what we do.

My first idea was to look for a new profession. I had been an engineer for over 30 years, and it was time to find something new, to redefine myself. So I became an ordained minister (thanks to the wonders of the internet). I quickly discovered being a minister was not much of a paying gig. Plus, I discovered the people who really needed what a minister provided could be a bit downtrodden – physically, emotionally, and/or spiritually. Go figure. Who would've ever guessed that? Well, I had issues dealing with people when they were at their *best*, so I certainly couldn't see myself dealing with people at their *worst*. Time to move on?

My second idea was to stand on a street corner holding a sign saying "Homeless. Need help", "Every little bit helps," or something along those lines, hand scrawled on a tattered piece of cardboard, complete with the requisite misspellings. Sounds like a bit of a rugged existence doesn't it? But I'm telling you, I've seen the guys on my street corner, and they were absolutely killing it. One guy wore $100+ Nike shoes on his feet and carried a brand new Swatch backpack slung over his shoulder. I had a steady paycheck for more than 30 years yet never once owned a $100 pair of Nikes. Maybe I was doing something wrong. Maybe my career choice was all wrong. I would need to give this holding of tattered cardboard signs some serious thought. In the end, sanity prevailed. After much careful consideration I opted not to go this route, primarily because of all the outdoor work required. Plus, there's that whole issue of having to deal with people, and there are probably local statutes that specifically prohibit impersonating a homeless dude. Again, time to move on.

My third idea was genius – start a GoFundMe site. Imagine just sitting at my desk clicking and typing, typing and clicking – not being exposed to the elements, not dealing with people. I mean all I had to do was say something about being an unemployed aerospace engineer, post a pathetic looking photo of myself on the site, and just sit back and watch the money roll in. That's how it works, right? Sweet. But then my conscience kicked in and wouldn't let me do it. Stupid conscience.

Well, after nixing serving as a minister, being a homeless dude, or starting a GoFundMe site, the only viable option left was writing a book. So here I am – an author. Note that exotic male dancer was another option I briefly considered and something I could've likely pulled off 20 years ago, but alas, no more.

But I had never been an author before, never written a book, never self-published a book. How does one do this? Good question. You just start, I learned.

In the process of writing this book I happened to stumble upon the book *The Subtle Art of Not Giving a F*ck*, by Mark Manson. As you will learn if you keep reading, I do not read very many books, so take this with a grain of salt, but that was the best book I have ever read. You have to deal with some rude language and expletives, but don't let that stop you from reading it. I found it both enlightening and confirming. And since it has sold over three million copies, apparently I'm not the only one who liked it.

One of my favorite lines in the book was related to the situation of finding yourself clueless about what to do next, *"Don't just sit there. Do something. The answers will follow."* In a similar vein, the following lines were also instructional:

> *"Life is about not knowing and then doing something anyway. All of life is like this. It never changes. Even when you're happy. Even when you're farting fairy dust. Even when you win the lottery and buy a small fleet of Jet Skis, you still won't know what the hell you're doing. Don't ever forget that. And don't be afraid of that either."*

So I did something. I wrote this book. Am I now happy? Well, I'm happy it's *done*, so there is that, but to my knowledge I haven't farted any fairy dust yet...

So please, read on. I hope you enjoy it. I welcome any comments you might have, directed to my email address: ronphillips.engineerstale@gmail.com.

CHAPTER 0
EXPECTATIONS

None. As in you should have absolutely no expectations about learning anything of value from this book. You should also have little to no expectations of coherency. The subtitle of this book is *Miscellaneous Ramblings...* for a good reason. Do not be surprised. I'm not leading anybody on. The word of the day here is *digress*.

One might think a highly educated and technical person such as myself would be able to write in a concise and understandable manner. One would think correctly. The difference here is money.

If you pay me a reasonable salary, then you will get coherent and understandable reports. I will try to lead the reader down a path of technical discovery, document each step along the way, and lay out all the assumptions and possible pitfalls of the analysis. In the end, hopefully the reader will be left with conclusions and recommendations that follow naturally from an exhaustive review of all available data. It's what engineers do. It's what separates engineers from the lesser apes, I suppose. (Plus engineers usually don't fling their poo when placed in confined spaces, like cubicles, for hours on end...)

However, if one is only willing to pay a few bucks for a paperback book, then *you get what you pay for*. In this case, exactly what the title implies, ramblings of a miscellaneous nature, infested with layers of digression. So, maybe money is what really separates engineers from the lesser apes?

Speaking of digressions, here is my first...

I have several credos that I developed or learned in my many years of dealing with humans. I have found credos are not typically required when dealing with animals, especially those of the small pet variety (cats, dogs, gerbils, tropical fish, etc.). Credos may, however, be required when dealing with animals that have both the desire and the capacity to hurt you and/or eat you.

Anyway, one of my early credos was "God didn't put me on this earth to give anybody a free living." To be honest, this was not so much a credo as much as just some rash bravado from me after a coworker asked if my wife was going to go back to work after the birth of our first child. Apparently I answered with such gusto that it became forever associated with me, thus a de facto credo. And not that I lived by that credo either, as my wife did eventually stay home and raise the kids. It was just all talk. In *True Grit* movie speak, it was the equivalent of Lucky Ned Pepper saying to Rooster Cogburn, "I call that pretty bold talk for a one-eyed fat man."

The ironic part is that now I am retired and my wife is still working, thus providing *me* with the free living. Good thing she didn't possess any strong need for credos to live by.

Similar to having credos, there are a host of general sayings and rules to live by (R2LB) which I shall insert sporadically at appropriate moments. Here are a few such examples:

R2LB: Never wrestle with a pig. You both get dirty and the pig likes it.
R2LB: The more you run over a dead cat, the flatter it gets.

Back on point, the credo that applies to the current situation, i.e. reading this book, is "keep your expectations low and you will not be disappointed." Those who know me have heard me say this often, which makes me think this entire discussion about credos is probably moot, since the only people who will likely purchase this book are friends, family, and co-workers who already know me. You see, I do live by my credos and thus keep my own expectations low. Note I will never ask you, the reader, to do something that I, the writer, would not be willing to do myself. That's not really a credo in and of itself, although it may sound a bit like one.

Back to my original point. If despite all my caveats and warnings mentioned above, you do choose to continue reading, then excellent. I'll make a deal with you. Keep your expectations of a good book low and I'll keep my expectations of selling many copies low as well. Agreed? It's a good thing you don't *need* this book for anything, and it's a good thing I don't *need* this book to put gas in the car, food on the table, or clothes on my back. We find ourselves in similar states, I suppose.

Continuing on? Good. I just hope I'm not giving too much away in this first introductory chapter.

My writing style is pretty much in-line with the KISS principle (Keep It Simple Stupid). [Please note there is a list of abbreviations, acronyms, and definitions at the back of the book.]

Remember, I'm an engineer by education and trade. When you fill your head with mathematics, equations, theories, proofs, integrals, derivatives and such, well there is just precious little room remaining for stuff like fine literature, or even good grammar for that matter. My mind is a zero sum game – nothing goes in without something coming out first. And spelling? Whew. If it weren't for computers with spell checking, I'd be *toost*. See what I did there? Another credo: I crack myself up (used so often that I have the acronym ICMU).

Here's a funny spell checking (or lack thereof) story, and this one isn't mine, but comes from a coworker with similar grammatical skills. In his report on the aerodynamic effect of carrying weapons on the F-15, the sentence should have read, "The F-15E has a wide variety of external *stores* that can be carried..." However, a simple typo combined with a non-engineering spell checker resulted in, "The F-15E has a wide variety of external *sores*..." I'm sure there are hundreds if not thousands of funnier spell checking stories, but I liked this one, it has a personal connection, and in any event I am the author here, so I get to choose. If you have a vast collection of humorous spell checking examples, then by all means write a book, get it published, and convince your family and friends to purchase it. It's a free country, or somewhat resembles one at times. Knock yourself out. Send me an email, I'll buy it.

Anyway, back to my writing style. The other not insignificant characteristic about me is that I cannot type very well. I first learned to type in my high school typing class, where half the class used manual typewriters and the other half (the lucky ones) got to use *electric* typewriters – yes, apparently, I am *that* old. Years later when computers first came on the scene, I was ill-prepared for so much keyboard work. What all of this means is if a word is more than say four or five characters long, then there is an almost certainty I will mistype at least one of those characters.

As a side note, in my non-Windows computer days of typing commands at a prompt (VAX VMS, UNIX, DOS) I would initially name my files *x*, as in *x.txt*, *x.dat*, etc. Why? Because there was a 75% chance I could type the single letter *x* without making a mistake, and I was all about going for the odds. I only had to hope once the file (or analysis using that file) was completed I would remember to go back and rename it to something more descriptive. Don't ask me how many times I forgot to do just that. Searching back in directories and finding a 10+ year old file named *x.dat* that I had absolutely no recollection of was just a part of my technical life. It's not unlike finding that unlabeled and undated container of *mystery meat* buried deep in your freezer. Do you dare eat it? Do I dare open that file?

In addition to me not typing well, my high school composition teacher instilled in me the notion of keeping writing simple, as opposed to waxing poetic for everything. Thus, another of my credos: "Never use a twenty-dollar word to make a one-dollar statement." For example, why use the word *enormous* when the word *big* or *huge* will work just as well? One might argue since there is a vast resource of words in our language, why not take advantage of them? Sorry, not for me. I'm writing neither poetry nor classic novels. I'm an engineer struggling mightily outside of my swim lane, as you shall no doubt see.

What all of this adds up to is if you see a big word and/or a lot of syllables, then either; a) I could not find a simpler word to use, or b) I'm trying to impress somebody – no doubt unsuccessfully.

I also made the conscious decision not to use footnotes for my many digressions and side stories. I recently read a book that employed copious (twenty-dollar word?) footnotes, so many in some cases the footnotes took more space on the page than the original text. I struggled to keep focus. I found if I didn't read the footnote text when and where it was marked, then it didn't flow as well or make as much sense. And if you have to read the footnote where marked, then you might as well just include it in the text, in my opinion. So I opted out. If you're one of those readers who loves separate footnotes, I apologize in advance.

One last comment about my writing style. My words are typically neither politically correct nor gender accurate. For example, when I use the word *guys* it is not limited to the male gender. I use it to simply mean a group of people. I'm not trying to offend or omit females in any way, as they are at times, a wonderful addition to the human race. When I was in college and later started working, the vast majority of engineers were male. Similarly, the vast majority of pilots were also male. Thus the term *guys* tended to cover most situations, say at least 90% of the time, which was better odds than I had at typing. Old habits die hard, I suppose.

I also use the word *kids* quite a bit. It is not meant to be a derogatory term, and I use it to lump together everybody under the age of say 25, which therefore includes most college age folks. Yes, I could say *children*, or *young adults*, but when I was growing up I was a *kid*, we were all *kids*, so *kids* it remains.

Enough about format and writing style? OK, on to the caveats.

If you read the back cover, then you know what I'm getting to here. The primary goal of this book is to demonstrate, via humor, why engineers *are* better than pilots. I suppose this quest is similar in nature to those humorous lists found on the internet, such as "Why a beer is better than a woman" or "25 reasons why dogs are better than men."

Is this book totally one-sided? Absolutely. By education and by trade, your author is an engineer, not a pilot. Would any different be expected from me? And while all of the stories in this book are true, was there, by chance, a bit of embellishment in the story telling at times? Again, absolutely. Would any different be expected from a light-hearted satire?

So, if you're looking for an *unbiased* answer to the question, "are engineers better than pilots?" you will not find it here. If you're looking for a pilot's perspective on this question, you will not find it here. If a pilot's perspective is what you really want, then I suppose you should; a) convince a pilot to write a book, and b) read that book.

I'll finish with an appropriate quote...

"People who take this seriously will be shot." – Mark Twain

CHAPTER 1
CHOOSING A CAREER

"Science can amuse and fascinate us all, but it is engineering that changes the world."
— Isaac Asimov

I was born in Everett, Washington (yes, where Boeing 747s were made). Not that my birthplace has anything much to do with either this book or my life, since we moved away when I was just six months old. My father was a fighter pilot in the Air Force, so we moved around quite a bit. After several years and multiple assignments, he opted to leave the Air Force to become an airline pilot for TWA, eventually settling down in Kansas City, Missouri, which is where the majority of my childhood was spent.

My father's career as a pilot forever shaped my future, if for no other reason than being surrounded by aircraft and pilots for my entire life. More to come on that later. Suffice it to say if it weren't for my father and his career choice, this book would not exist, and that would be sad. Sad, because you'd have nothing to do right now. You'd be sitting in your favorite chair, bored, wondering if there were any good books to read.

Youngest of three children. Normal childhood growing up in the Midwest. I assume *normal*. But what is normal? How does one know? I grew up. Attended public schools. Took piano lessons. Boy Scout. Built plastic models. Rode my bike. Freckled. Family shopped at Kmart. Terribly awkward around girls. That was my résumé. Was it possible to get any more *normal* than that?

You might have noted the absence of *sports* or *physical stature* on my childhood résumé. With the lone exception of my kindergarten year, I was always the *smallest* kid in the class. Typically also the *slowest* kid in the class. Not a great combination. The *double* curse. I was, however, a bright student. In reality, with little to no hope of being good at sports, what other choice was there? Note that a sport favoring the small and the slow had not yet been developed in the 1960s, at least none that I was aware of.

As a result of my early life *predicament*, I developed one of my earliest credos: "Every person needs to have at least *one* redeeming quality." Note simply being a human being on this planet did <u>not</u> qualify as that one redeeming quality. God may love us. Our mothers might even love us. But that didn't mean everybody else on this planet didn't know us to be self-absorbed, obnoxious, pretentious, bigoted jerks with no special skills or aptitude, just as an example.

While good grades were earned in all my school classes, my *interests* gravitated towards math and science. (Well, *some* science – Chemistry was loathsome, for some unknown reason.) Becoming an engineer, thus, might have seemed like a foregone conclusion. However, for many years I thought I wanted to be a pilot, like my father. Two discoveries and two physicalities disavowed me of that notion forever.

But first, a pilot joke...

Son, you're going to have to make up your mind about growing up and becoming a pilot. You can't do both.

Discovery number one was witnessing my dad hanging out with his pilot buddies on multiple occasions. You would have been amazed at how much these guys could talk, and just how arrogant they sounded. One pilot would start off a conversation about some great personal aerial exploit. Another pilot would jump in, cutting him off, and talking louder. Then a third pilot would interrupt both of them, at an even higher volume. And thus the cycle of ratcheting bravado and volume would ensue. It was the equivalent of the "Are too! Am not!" playground argument of our youth, except this was between grown men. Add to that the constant use of hands and arms to help illustrate their aerial exploit trajectories and you had a pretty comedic scene of dog-fighting prowess one-upmanship.

Think of the view from an outside observer – even from a distance far enough to not hear the actual words spoken, you would see three mouths open simultaneously and six arms flailing in the air. To my recollection, a pilot never actually *won* one of these arguments. But maybe that was not the point, was it? Maybe just being *in the fight* was satisfaction enough? Don't know. I do know an eight year old boy came away with an altered perspective of his father and of pilots.

Hang on, another pilot joke...

Q: How many fighter pilots does it take to change a light bulb?
A: Just one. He holds the bulb in place and waits for the world to revolve around him.

Discovery number two was of a more technical nature. I built countless model airplanes as a kid. I know what you might be thinking... Yes, we are products of our environment, and yes, that environment included the aroma of model cement, and yes, that may explain a lot. Sure. Anyway, yes, *countless* models. As soon as sufficient allowance was earned it was blown purchasing yet another model. When visiting my grandparents in Atlanta every summer, *Granny* would take my brother and me to Kmart and buy us, you guessed it, a model. Staying home *sick* from school was a treat because it conveniently wasn't much of a physical strain to sit at my desk and build models. Ahem... cough... cough. (Had I not had such a passion for building models, I might've gotten perfect attendance awards in school.) My parents would often come to my room and ask if I wanted to join the family downstairs, watching some TV program. Umm. No. If engineering was to consume my adult life (and it did), then building model airplanes would consume my childhood.

Be all that as it may, I busied myself with gluing and painting aircraft models, all the while studying their unique shapes, sizes, and features. Intrigued. Why unique? Why so different?

My dad flew several fighter types in the USAF (F-86 Sabre, F-100 Super Sabre, and the F-102 Delta Dart). Anybody could see that each of these aircraft was unique in shape, but *why*? They were all fighters, right? So, I asked, "Hey Dad, why does the F-100 have a swept wing and horizontal tail, but the F-102 has a delta wing with no tail?" He replied, "Dunno." Undaunted, I tried again, "Hey Dad, why does the F-86 have a single inlet in the nose, but the F-102 has dual inlets on the fuselage sides, especially since both have just one engine?" "Dunno," yet again. Hmm. Was there a pattern here?

Ahh, the cloud was lifting – pilots don't necessarily know anything about how airplanes are *designed*. They may know how to *operate* them, i.e. stick, throttles, pedals, buttons, and levers, but knowing *how* to fly an airplane in no way implied any knowledge of *why* it looked or behaved like it did. I don't know why this was such a revelation to me. I mean, millions of people, including myself, drive cars without having a clue how to design or build one. The same can be said for toilets, I suppose.

That was my turning point. The end game. Knowing *why* airplanes looked the way they did. Knowing *why* airplanes flew the way they did. Anybody could *fly* an airplane, or so I thought at the time, but I wanted to *design* an airplane. With engineering already set as my career choice due to my natural inclination towards math and science, *Aerodynamics* would become my obvious focus. Conversely, I had no such inclination or focus regarding toilets.

Fast forward for a moment to my college days. After studying engineering for a few years, the topics of kinematic and inertial coupling were introduced. The two poster child aircraft for the discovery of kinematic and inertial coupling effects were the F-100 and the F-102. "Hey, what luck, my Dad flew both of these aircraft. He'll certainly know a bit about this," I thought.

Son: "Hey Dad, what was inertial coupling like in the F-100 and F-102?"
Father: "What? Coupling? Uhhh. I dunno."

Apparently, the right career choice had been made. Sometimes in life you get confirmation on things even when you didn't ask for it. Thanks, Dad.

Family photo in front of my dad's F-100, McConnell AFB, KS, circa 1968. I believe my older sister took the photo. Cute kids, huh? Nice black socks, Ron. Classy.

Photo of my father and his F-100 while stationed at Kunsan AFB in Korea, circa 1968. How could anyone possibly look at this photo and *not* want to be a fighter pilot when they grew up?

Photo of my father (right) while stationed in Korea, circa 1968. The other guy (with the same name) was an F-4 pilot stationed in South Vietnam.

Seems like an appropriate time for another pilot joke...

Fighter Pilots: Cold, steely eyed, weapons systems managers who kill bad people and break things. However, they can also be very charming and personable. The average fighter pilot, despite sometimes having a swaggering exterior, is very much capable of such feelings as love, affection, intimacy, and caring. These feelings generally just don't involve anyone else.

CHAPTER 2
OFF TO COLLEGE

"The first duty of the university is to teach wisdom, not a trade; character, not technicalities. We want a lot of engineers in the modern world, but we do not want a world of engineers."
   – Winston Churchill

Growing up in Kansas City and in such close proximity to Wichita, Kansas – the self-proclaimed aeronautical center of the universe – it seemed like a no-brainer I would attend Wichita State University. Ever since I was about eight years old, I knew that was my future. This is in stark contrast with most kids these days, who make it to college without knowing what they really want to do in life. I simply could not grasp the concept of going to college without knowing. Realize that thousands upon thousands of kids do just that and turn out fine, it just wasn't in my DNA. To each his own, I suppose.

During my senior year in high school, when the college search process started in earnest, two new but important concepts surfaced: *out-of-state* tuition and *scholarship* money. Wichita State was in Kansas. I was a Missouri resident. In effect, Wichita, while only 200 miles from KC, might as well have been in Sri Lanka. Paying out-of-state tuition was essentially out of the question.

During that year my guidance counselor told me Missouri had an engineering school, located in the small town of Rolla, about 100 miles southwest of St. Louis. Rolla? Huh, never heard of it. He also informed me that due to my high class standing, the state of Missouri would offer me a scholarship to cover 100% of my tuition expenses for four full years. Some quick research revealed Rolla did in fact offer a degree in *Aerospace Engineering*, among many others. Done deal. Decision could not have been easier. Dad took me and two of my high school friends to Rolla for a campus visit, but in effect, it was just a courtesy trip, as I had already made up my mind. Or more accurately, the reality of dollars and cents had made up my mind. Regardless of what I would see or not see during my campus visit, I was destined to be a *Rolla boy*.

Oh yeah, I almost forgot, two physicalities...

Unknown to me at the tender age of eight, but now learned, was the Air Force and Navy had little things called *minimum physical requirements*, and these had to be met to be accepted as a pilot trainee. As it turned out, they preferred candidates to be at least 5'6" tall and have at least 20-40 *uncorrected* vision. Who knew? Well crap. None of the above. Short, slow, *and* myopic. The *triple* curse. *Military aviator* was simply out of reach, even if desired (more to follow).

The Navy told me they would accept lower physical standards (via waivers) for navigators and *back seat* guys, and offered a nice full-ride scholarship, plus living expenses, based solely on my academic record. However, accepting that Navy scholarship was a *commitment*. No free lunches from the Navy. Signing that form would've bequeathed the next *eleven* years of my life to the Navy – four in college followed by a seven year service commitment. I had no problems with the military. I was an Air Force brat. I loved the military and all things military related. But this seventeen year old teenager did not feel at ease signing a piece of paper that would've pre-determined the next decade of my life.

Then there was also that little thing about... *water*. *Strong swimmer* was also nowhere to be found on my childhood résumé. Sure, *Swimming* Merit Badge was earned while a Boy Scout, but I came close to drowning in the process. Me and deeper than bathtub water were not bosom buddies. Short, slow, myopic, *and* a dog paddler. The *quadruple* curse?

Not that I needed more data points, but the movie *Jaws* came out in 1975. Remember? I do. Our family saw it on the big screen. I was thirteen years old. Absolutely scared the crap out of me. From that day forward I was convinced every square mile of the world's oceans were teeming with hundreds of great white sharks whose sole purpose in life was to eat me. Yes, the rational budding engineer in me knew it wasn't possible for an ocean to have *that* many great white sharks, but this was no place for rational thought.

There you have it. No more data points required. God was telling me, and not so subtly, the Navy was not for me. In church we were taught two things: God has a plan for each of us, and God works in mysterious ways. It was clear, God wanted me to be a Rolla boy. A plan? Yes. Mysterious? Hmm, not sure. In any event, I heeded His advice.

You may wonder, why all this contemplation of Air Force and Navy, when I plainly stated that by age eight I knew I wanted to be an engineer? One reason; the discovery that you could do *both*, i.e. you could earn an engineering degree *and* be in the military. Upon graduation with an engineering degree, pilot training was a quite feasible career path. Intriguing. I could be an *educated* pilot. I still feared non-acceptance based on the minimum physical requirements – i.e. my prospects of growing two inches taller and gaining perfect eyesight during college were slim at best. And maybe that was the mysterious way God operated? Not only did He want me to go to Rolla, but He also was going to make sure I couldn't become a pilot. His plan for me, again not so subtly, was for me to become an engineer. It was time to stop resisting.

It is interesting now to reflect back on those decisions. What if I had been two inches taller? What if I had better vision? What if I could swim better? Would I have opted for the military aviator route? Would I have made it through pilot training?

Going back even further, what if my dad never chose to become a pilot? Was I an aviation nut because my dad was a pilot, or was aviation in my blood? It's the age-old question of environment versus heredity, I suppose. But what if my dad had become an accountant instead of a pilot? I can't imagine a young boy witnessing three CPAs having a one-upmanship argument about their *fiscal computing prowess* or their *fiduciary exploits*, complete with hands waving in the air. But had that happened, would I have become a nerd accountant instead of a nerd engineer?

Lots of questions. No answers. So, let's cut the daydreaming and get back to the matter at hand – college.

Graduating from high school required a minimal amount of effort. Some won't like to hear this, but public school was not much of a challenge for me (and many of my friends). Letter grades of A's were earned, but rarely was a book taken home to study. Homework was generally completed during free time at school, and exams were typically not difficult enough to require much time spent studying at home. Accelerated courses were taken when available, which proved a bit more challenging, but not insurmountable with just a little more effort. This was all because I was smart, right? The truth would be learned soon enough.

Fall arrives and I'm off to Rolla – more correctly known as University of Missouri Rolla (UMR) at the time. Now it is known as Missouri Institute of Science and Technology (MoST). (We humorous engineers like to use the acronym MoIST, for obvious reasons.) Before UMR, it was known as the Missouri School of Mines (MSM). Kind of like companies reorganizing every few years in an attempt to feign progress, some colleges feel the need to rename themselves at certain intervals, I suppose. Whatever. As long as you get a degree and a company gives you a job, do you care if you attended a *School*, or a *College*, or a *University*, or an *Institute*? Me neither.

With no prior college experience, there was little realization that the facilities at UMR were, in reality, kind of a dump. My dorm, Kelly Hall, was pre–WW2 construction; with concrete floors, no A/C, and a central boiler plant providing steam heating that was not turned on until *after* Thanksgiving break, regardless of the outside temperature. The mess hall food was terrible. The term *freshman fifteen*, meaning one gains fifteen pounds during their freshman year, was not coined until well after my college years, I suppose. Freshman year was a weight loss clinic. Many times cold cereal for three meals a day were consumed because what was offered for lunch and dinner simply could not be stomached. When tired of cold cereal, a switch to cinnamon toast was made. Mercifully, the cafeteria left milk, cereal, bread, and toasters available all day.

The campus itself was nothing to write home about – many old buildings with creaky floors and rattling windows. And coming from KC, the relatively small town of Rolla was also nothing to write home about. I say *relatively*, because Rolla was considered by many to be the *big* town in this part of Missouri. For some people, Rolla was a town to visit on occasion for shopping and dining – a *destination* city, as it were. In the grand scheme of things, attending college in a small town with little else to do was a blessing, as it afforded essentially no distractions from the primary mission – to study and earn an engineering degree. Rolla filled that bill nicely.

Sounds like complaining? Not really. At the time I didn't know the place was a dump – it was all I knew, my new home, and fine with me. The university had a solid academic reputation, and the degree program was rigorous. Nothing was handed to you; every grade had to be *earned*. That was the important matter at hand; everything else was a side issue. So, when saying UMR was a *dump*, it is in the context of me attending the school in the early 1980s and now writing this in 2019, after visiting other gorgeous campuses like Stanford and Notre Dame, and taking college campus trips with my three children, all long after my graduation from UMR. To be fair, the MoST campus and facilities of today are nothing like the UMR campus of the 1980s. College is simply not the same as it was 30+ years ago, and this is likely true of just about any campus. And Rolla is a very nice town.

Anyway, back to the 1980s when I was a *smart* kid, or rather thought I was. My years of rarely if ever having to study in high school left me woefully unprepared for college, or at least for pursuing an engineering degree at UMR. I can't speak to other schools or degrees, but I assume it would've been similar elsewhere. The first semester at UMR absolutely kicked my butt. Prior to starting college, I had visions of sleeping late, attending class for a few hours, playing golf or tennis, studying a little bit, playing card games until bedtime, and then going home on most weekends. Visions have never been more wrong.

The harsh reality was: woke early, ate breakfast (cereal), studied, went to class, studied, ate lunch (more cereal), went to class and/or labs, studied more, ate dinner (even more cereal), and then studied until bedtime. Next day, same routine. Rinse. Repeat. Weekends, once the harbinger of lazy free time, were now crammed with studying in order to simply *survive* the upcoming week. After a semester of spending essentially every waking hour either in class or studying, all I could manage for grades was one A and three B's. This was crushing to the all A's high school student with a full tuition scholarship. Biggest shock of my life. Nothing, absolutely nothing, in the forty years of my life since has topped that first semester for shock value. I kid you not. It probably didn't help during that first semester my parents announced they were getting divorced and my high school girlfriend dumped me. But those were not the real reasons for my less than expected academic performance, and I knew it.

The truly depressing part was the first year or so of an engineering degree typically consisted of the *basic* courses. Ostensibly most of the *hard* stuff was still to come. Holy shit. The number one thing learned that first semester was not math or science, but that I simply did not know *how* to study. The other equally depressing part was noticing other students, many *without* scholarships, who were not struggling. Somehow or somewhere, those other kids had learned how to study. One can only assume they had to work hard for good grades in high school, and thus had mastered the requisite techniques. (It is worth noting there were four of us highly ranked students from my high school that attended UMR together, and we all struggled similarly at the beginning, so it wasn't just me.) Anyway, since most courses were graded on a curve, it meant we were competing against those students who did know how to study.

The other *education* about engineering school was that it was not a touchy-feely kind of place. Neither the administration nor the faculty were overly interested in your success or your failure. They were not your friends, they had not seen you grow up, they did not know your parents, and your home town meant nothing to them. You were a student ID number, a seat in their classroom, and a grade to be processed each semester. Most classrooms were overly full, so the more people that couldn't cut it and dropped out, well, the easier it was for the faculty to handle the course load. That was the reality. I suppose the question is, was that the *incentive*? The professors had to maintain some office hours for students to ask questions if they were having difficulties, but to be honest until reaching upper level courses in my major, I seldom found my professors to be very eager to help. As a freshman, it was intimidating to walk into a professor's office, and the impression was that was the way the professors liked it.

The bottom line was the first two years or so of college truly were sink or swim. In my aerospace engineering (AE) degree program, we had 150+ students in my freshman intro class. Five years later, my graduating class had only around 30 people. The saying going around campus was, "look to your left, look to your right, only one of you will be around at graduation." Too bad the reality was, at least in my degree program, "look *two* to your left, look *two* to your right..."

Attrition was the name of the game. In my Heat Transfer course, the semester started with forty students. After the mid-term exam it was down to *twenty* students. When the semester ended there were *eight* of us left standing. And by the way, Heat Transfer was a *required* course for a mechanical or aerospace engineering degree. So, in my, albeit limited, one class sample size, there were 32 students who either had to retake (and ultimately pass) Heat Transfer or find another degree program.

That first Heat Transfer exam kicked my butt, which was becoming an all too common theme for me. The professor handed back our tests. I got a score of 40% – not even *half* of the problems correct. Visibly shaken, the exam paper was quickly turned face down on my desk so nobody could see it. Too embarrassed. The professor then wrote all the test scores on the board, so the distribution was out in the open. Amazed. Stunned. That piece of crap 40% score was the *highest* in the class. In terms of grades, you could live by the curve, but could also die by the curve. I survived to fight another day.

No complaints about the apparent lack of caring or emotional support during my college years. Weeding out those who could not compete was the right thing to do – especially since the alternative would be to keep them in the program, keep taking their tuition money away from them, and then have them either fail in their junior or senior years, or worse, graduate but not be able to get a job. Sink or swim worked in my opinion. It just had to be understood and accepted that many people would indeed sink. That possibility certainly lit a fire under my butt. I simply couldn't fail, as I was too damn short and too blind to fall back on being a pilot.

[Author's note: I have heard in the years since the 1980s that UMR and other schools have become more helpful for students who struggle with their course work. I understand they offer more assistance, including tutoring and counseling. I would hope and assume this is for the benefit of the student. However, I worry that keeping a struggling student in a program they may not be able to master will not serve them well in the long run. I also worry the school's motivation to keep struggling students is primarily to keep their tuition payments flowing. Every person is not cut out to get every degree or perform every job; I hope we have not lost sight of that fact.]

So, Ron, you thought you would just sneak in that *five years later...* comment, didn't you? Gee, Ron, why did it take you *five* years to get a *four*-year degree? Perhaps because you never actually learned *how* to study? Nice try, but not the case here. I worked as a co-op student with McDonnell Douglas (MDC) in St. Louis while in school. Co-op students alternated semesters working then attending school, so in the end it took an extra year to complete the degree program. For me, the experience gained and the money earned while working every other semester was well worth the additional time it took to graduate. No sneaking here. Full disclosure.

One co-op side story...

During my final co-op session, prior to my senior year, I was assigned to the F-15 aerodynamics group. One of my tasks was to run computer simulations of takeoffs, the results of which would be included in the Flight Manual in the form of predicted takeoff speeds and distances. One morning my supervisor, Bill, informed me that our Branch Chief, Clarence, wanted to discuss with me that afternoon what I was working on and what the results were. Huh? A Branch Chief was the *second highest* position in the entire department, why would he possibly want to talk with me, a co-op student, who hadn't even completed a degree yet? Regardless of the rationale, Bill had arranged for me to meet with him at one o'clock that afternoon.

The rest of the morning was spent preparing for the upcoming meeting. A few minutes before the prescribed meeting time, I collected my data, plots, and graphs, and started down the aisle. Passing by Bill's desk, he stopped me and said, "Good luck, Ron," with a smirk on his face. No clue what the smirk was about, but I replied, "Thanks, Bill."

While the rest of us peon engineers sat in a large, open bullpen array of desks, Branch Chiefs had real offices with real doors. I approached Clarence's real office, found his real door open, and noticed that nobody was inside talking with him. I gently rapped on the door, entered, and started talking, "Hey Clarence, Bill said you wanted to discuss my takeoff simulation results. What I have so far..." Stopped. Mid-sentence. His eyes were closed. He may have been sitting upright in his chair, but he was most assuredly *asleep*.

Frozen, with no clue how to proceed. I didn't want to do anything *loud*, like a fake clearing of my throat, to startle him awake, because of the potential embarrassment of him opening his eyes and seeing me standing but two feet away. What was the protocol for this situation, pray tell? Retreating back to the real door, I briefly contemplated knocking *hard*, but then chickened out and retreated further, out of the office and back to my aisle. If this were World Cup Soccer, the score would read: Sleeping Branch Chief 1. Cowardly co-op student 0.

Ashen faced and stunned, I approached Bill's desk, sorely needing his guidance regarding what to do next. He's already chuckling and says, "How did it go, Ron?" All that could be mustered was a whisper, "He's *asleep*." Bill, along with several others within earshot, burst into laughter. One of the other engineers quipped, "It's after lunch. *Of course* Clarence is asleep." More laughter.

I had been set up. Everybody in the group *knew* Clarence took a siesta every afternoon. Everybody in the group *knew* not to schedule meetings with Clarence right after lunch. Everybody but me. After the hilarity had subsided, and some quality nap time has passed, Bill himself walked me back to Clarence's real office, rapped on the real door, and introduced the topic we were to discuss. Clarence was a new man. Awake. Alert. Rejuvenated. We had a very nice discussion.

During my senior year in college, it was time to start looking for a permanent job. Three things were known for certain: I wanted to work in Aerodynamics, I wanted to work on fighter aircraft, and I did not want to live on the east or west coasts. Proud product of the Midwest; I *liked* the Midwest. In my mind, the east and west coast cities were great places to visit while on vacation, but to be avoided as a permanent residence.

An interview with General Dynamics in Fort Worth, TX was arranged. Note an interview with MDC in St. Louis had already occurred, more on that later. Texas was not really in the Midwest per se, but was a reasonable alternative to the left and right coasts. After receiving respectable offers from both companies, in the end I decided to work for MDC on the F-15 program. My final co-op work session had been with the F-15 Aerodynamics group at MDC, as mentioned earlier, so I was already familiar with the people and the work.

Graduation ceremonies at UMR were on a Thursday, I believe. Work at MDC started the following Monday. Many people would take several weeks or even months off after graduation before starting work, and more than a few of them thought I was nuts for starting work so soon. One good reason – money. Or lack thereof, more specifically. At the time of graduation, my checking account balance was 25 *cents*. Those old enough to remember know there was no such thing as free checking back then. No, fees had to be paid for the mere *privilege* of having a checking account, and without the benefit of earning interest either, I might add. For my wonderfully accommodating bank, the fees happened to be 15 cents per month plus 10 cents per check written. So, *flat broke* would arrive after one more month and one more check. Clarity introduced herself to me yet again. No decision process required. I needed money and I needed it now. Hi ho, hi ho, it's off to work I go...

Ron

Before I start talking about work, I've got several Rolla stories to share...

Toilets...

Remember I mentioned my dorm, Kelly Hall, was pre-WW2 construction? Well, that also meant it featured pre-WW2 bathroom facilities. The predominant *feature*, to say it politely, was a total lack of privacy. When you walked into the door (which was always propped open for ease of entry) there was immediately a row of urinals. And you know those little divider walls they sometimes put in between each urinal? Yeah, no. None of those. Just behind the row of urinals was a row of sinks, so a guy standing at the sink would look up into the mirror and see his reflection, but could also see a row of guys standing at the urinals.

Next to that was another section, with another row of sinks (sharing the same wall as the other sinks). Just behind those sinks was a row of toilets. Those toilets did have divider walls, but no doors. So, similar to the other side, a guy standing at the sink would look up into the mirror and see his reflection, but could also see a row of guys sitting down, facing him, while taking care of business. A most pleasant atmosphere with which to brush one's teeth or shave one's face.

The third section of the bathroom was the shower stall. Note I said *stall*, not *stalls*. It was a community shower with one big open room with seven shower nozzles protruding, two from either end, and three from the longer center wall. In the mornings it was a pretty busy place, with a lot of the guys trying to get ready for a day of classes – six guys showering at one time (only *six* because the seventh nozzle never worked). So, in the mornings, one had to stand in line and wait for a shower nozzle to become available.

You know those little things called *anti-scald* water valves? Yeah, no. We had none of those. Every time a toilet was flushed, it took cold water away from the showers, and if you weren't prepared for it then you got a slug of very hot water for a few moments. The most typical way to reach the state of *preparedness* was to get scalded once, then come to understand why each guy instinctively stepped away from the nozzle whenever he heard a toilet flush.

17

While waiting in line, whenever you heard a toilet flush, you would see six guys, many of them lathered up and eyes closed, take a step to the middle and then a step back, all in unison. Think synchronized swimming. Or better yet, think square dancing. Each toilet flush was like the caller announcing the next step, in this case a do-si-do. And at each flush you would see six guys doing the do-si-do in unison. And note that flushing toilets was a very common occurrence at that busy time in the morning, so your typical 4-5 minute shower might require a dozen or so do-si-do maneuvers.

It was all actually pretty amusing. Not that watching six guys taking a shower was amusing. And not that we in the queue were staring intently or anything, but if you were first in line, you had to pay attention, didn't you? Just like driving a car and being first in line at a stoplight, you had to pay attention so you would know when the light turned green and it was OK to proceed. And you knew, when it was your turn in the shower, that all those guys still in the queue would be the ones watching you do-si-do to the *music* of the flushing toilets. Now, had those flushing toilets ever called for a promenade, *that* would have been amusing.

Possibly the most interesting part, looking back, is that nobody complained about the bathroom layout, the showers, or the utter lack of any privacy. It's just the way it was and we all lived with it.

Toilets – part deux

Because of the layout of the dorm quad, my Kelly Hall first floor hallway was a well-traveled path. People from all of the dorms quickly discovered that it was easier to walk *through* Kelly Hall rather than walk all the way *around* Kelly Hall.

One weekend in the spring of my freshman year there was an open house, or some sort of family day event, or whatever – I was too busy studying to know what was going on around me. Anyway, it was a Saturday morning and I got out of bed around 9 AM or so, threw on a bathrobe and flip-flops, and shuffled down to the bathroom. As I'm standing at the urinals taking care of business (yes, bathroom door still propped open for ease of entry), a prospective UMR student, along with his parents, grandparents, and younger sisters, sauntered by. And, human nature being what it is, they couldn't help but peek *into* the open doorway. Remember, no divider walls at the urinals. All I could do was turn my head and smile at my newfound audience. Welcome to Rolla, dude. Hmm, I wonder if he opted for a different university? I wonder if I played some role in that decision making process?

Toilets – part trois

You might be wondering how I kept so calm, cool, and collected standing at the urinal with all those on-lookers? One word. Experience. Back in high school one of the favorite hangouts was a run-down bar in Kansas called *Wild Bill Cody's*. Kansas? Yes, because the drinking age in Missouri was 21, but only 18 in Kansas. Anyway, the bar provided all that we needed, i.e. live country music, a dance floor, and cheap beer.

The guy's bathroom was a small closet of a room containing a toilet, a urinal, a sink, and three guys peeing non-stop. I'm going to let that sink in for a moment. *Three* guys peeing (note I was too short to, ahem, *reach* the sink). There were also no dividers or stalls, so every time the door swung open for somebody to enter or exit, the three pee guys were in plain sight. And this was a bar serving cheap beer, by the pitcher, to high school students, so as you might imagine that door swung open countless times every night.

The girl's bathroom was just down the hall from the guy's bathroom. There was always a long line of girls waiting for that bathroom, and that line just happened to wind around right by the door to the guy's bathroom. So, yes, every time the door swung open, the three pee guys were effectively *on display* for the lucky girls who happened to be in line at that location.

One time, while I was one of the three, a guy swung the door open, apparently one too many times, and it came crashing down. The hinges had broken. That was my first introduction to metal fatigue. Did we three guys stop peeing? No. Did the lucky girls in line stop looking? No. Did the proprietors of the bar fix the door? No. Did I have to make several more trips to the bathroom that night? Yes. I was a short, slow, myopic, dog paddler with a small bladder. The *quintuple* curse?

OK, that's probably way too much discussion about toilets. I'd better change the subject or you might begin to think I'm fixated or something. Sorry.

Big red Calculus book...

While walking back from campus during finals week, I saw a guy come out of the Chemical Engineering (ChemE) building, where a Calculus final had just finished. He was not a happy camper, to say the least. He threw his book to the ground in disgust. And instead of regaining his composure and picking the book back up, he kicked it all the way from the ChemE building back to the dorms at the quad – a distance of several hundred yards, spewing expletives along the way.

This was no average textbook. This was the big red Calculus book. It was thick. It was heavy. This book was good for three full semesters of Calculus. This book costs $50. Yes, *fifty* dollars. It may not sound like much today, but back in 1979 that was a lot of money. For some perspective, most new textbooks back then cost about $10-20, so $50 for a single book was an inordinate amount of money. For a bit more perspective, prior to college I worked a summer job at Sears and made $2.35 per hour. It took forty hours of work (after taxes) to pay for that single book. Total tuition for the semester at UMR was only around $400 – for a full course load. I hope you can see that $50 was not a trivial amount.

So anyway, here is this guy kicking his $50 big red Calculus book halfway across campus. The rest of us bystanders were in total shock and awe. It wasn't even funny. It's something that *should* have been funny, but was not. It was just sad. No doubt that guy did not come back to UMR the following year. He probably didn't like the bathroom facilities either, I suppose.

What's in a Name?

Early in my college career I had to take one Computer Science (CompSci) course. It taught us basic programming skills. FORTRAN was the language at the time. And back in those days there were no personal computers, but rather a huge mainframe sitting on the first level of the CompSci building. We also used punch cards to enter our lines of code and data. FORTRAN? Mainframe? Punch cards? I say this quite often, but yes, apparently I am that old.

Anyway, the process was you would figure out the code in your head, type it into the punch card machine, hit ENTER, and watch the cards zip into and out of the machine (hanging chad anyone?). Then you would organize the cards in proper order and take them to the card reader operator (typically a freshman CompSci major trying to earn a few extra dollars). Within a few minutes your job would run on the mainframe and, if successful, your output would print out on a large fan-fold printer. Another freshman CompSci major had the glorious job of tearing off fan-fold output every so often, and then sorting through it to separate each individual job (each person's job had a header sheet with their last name printed in large letters). That stack of now separated printer output was then handed to yet another freshman CompSci major whose job it was to sort them into bins alphabetically. We budding programmers would wait patiently at the output window and wait for our job to compile, run, print, separate, and sort. Then we would review our output, fix the errors, and repeat the cycle (nothing ever worked the first time).

So, one day I walked up to the output window and the CompSci dude asked me, "Last name?" I answered, "Phillips." Dude came back with, "Is that with a Ph?" Huh? At that point in my life I had been a *Phillips* for almost twenty years and had never, not once, known anybody with that same last name spelled with an F. How could it be anything other than *Ph*? In addition, UMR had thousands of students, many of them from foreign countries with all manner of odd sounding and/or spelled last names, and this guy had problems with *Phillips*? Wow.

"Yes, Ph." Note, had I been on top of my game I would've had some snarky comeback like, "No, Phillips with a *silent Z*", or something along those lines, just to torment the dude. But alas, I was young, naïve, and not that quick-witted. In fact, snarkiness was something that took years of working in the Aerospace industry to develop...

UMR basketball game...

UMR was a small Division II school, so sports weren't a huge deal on campus. During my freshman and sophomore years, however, we actually had competitive football and basketball teams, and I went to as many of the home games as possible. One particular Friday night we had a home basketball game against Central Missouri State University (CMSU), and the gym was packed – more on that later. Three funnies from this game.

Number 1. At one point in the game, there was a dubious foul called against one of the UMR players. The stands erupted in a chorus of boos. FYI – a gym full of frustrated engineering students does not make for a sportsmanlike crowd. There was a student in the stands dressed up like a referee with a black and white striped uniform, but he wore dark sunglasses and carried a blind person's cane. After the call, he ran onto the court and stumbled around, pretending to be a blind ref. The chorus of boos changed to a cacophony of laughter. He was soon escorted off the court and out of the gym, but the damage, or *entertainment*, had already been done.

Number 2. The gym was unusually packed, partly because it was a Friday night game in a town where there was precious little to do on weekends, but primarily because CMSU brought their cheerleading squad. CMSU was a liberal arts college in close proximity to Kansas City. UMR also had a cheerleading squad, but just not of the same caliber, for several reasons. One reason was CMSU had a much higher enrollment than Rolla. Another was because the girl to guy ratio at Rolla was only about 1:7, but much more balanced at CMSU. And yet another was cheerleaders didn't tend to flock to small schools in rural Missouri to pursue engineering degrees. Sorry if that sounds a bit harsh, but it was just reality. Suffice it to say CMSU had a much larger pool of coeds to draw from when it came time to fielding a cheerleading squad.

At halftime the CMSU cheerleaders took center court and performed a routine complete with a *five* layer human pyramid. At the end of the routine the cheerleader at the top of the pyramid fell blindly backwards and two guys caught her. Pretty impressive. You've no doubt seen similar, right? The crowd gave the away team squad a boisterous standing ovation.

Then the UMR cheerleading squad took center court. They performed a comparatively unremarkable routine with a *three* layer human pyramid. At the end of the routine the cheerleader on top fell backwards and the guys actually *dropped* her. Thankfully she wasn't hurt (not that far of a fall), but sheesh. No boisterous applause. No standing ovation. I'm guessing you *haven't* seen similar?

Number 3. The score of the game was close, with leads changing hands frequently. Near the end of the game, one side called time out with 2:09 left on the clock. The stands erupted in a chorus of "Two-Oh-Nine... Two-Oh-Nine..." You see, Rolla had a bar located at 209 Pine Street that was generally known only as *209*, a place, by the way, where many *fluids* labs were held (sorry for the inside joke). The CMSU fans in the stands had absolutely no clue what was going on, which made it all the more humorous for us *in the know*.

Engineering humor – it's an acquired taste, I suppose.

My then future wife and I met during college, while we were both working as co-op students at MDC. She was working towards a mechanical engineering degree at Purdue University, in Indiana. As one may surmise, many of my friends and family members were shocked to learn I actually *had* a girlfriend (shocked for more than one reason, I'm sure). Time and time again the question was exclaimed to me, "You went to Rolla and found a *girlfriend*?" Oh heavens no, with a girl to guy ratio of only 1:7, I had to *import* mine from Purdue.

Engineering humor indeed. And now there were *two* of us.

CHAPTER 3
MY FIRST ASSIGNMENT

"Aviation is the branch of engineering that is least forgiving of mistakes."
   – Freeman Dyson

I showed up for work on my first day and was told to go home, or more correctly, to go home and come back later that evening. I was assigned to the *Advanced* F-15 aerodynamics group, not the regular F-15 group, as I was expecting. They had just started a two-shift wind tunnel test at the MDC Polysonic Wind Tunnel (PSWT) in St. Louis and needed *help* covering the second shift. The term *help* is used very loosely here, as a fresh out of college engineer on his first day, such as myself, was about as useless as ejection seats in a helicopter.

I knew *nothing*. I knew *how* to do *nothing*. This was a bit of a shock to me, having just graduated near the top of my class with an aerospace engineering degree from a *prestigious* university (defined as at least one-third of the population in southeast Missouri had heard of the town *Rolla*). Add to that being a co-op student who had worked for a summer in the Aerodynamics department at MDC. Nothing? How could I possibly know nothing? That was the start of my *Engineering Realization* (ER) collection, i.e. tidbits of wisdom picked up along my career.

ER: Humility is a wonderful thing. New engineers don't know shit. Accept it. Get over yourselves. Engineering school taught you generically *how* to think and *how* to tackle problems. The ins and outs of your specific job will be learned by listening to and watching experienced engineers ply their trade.

Maybe Einstein said it better?
   "Education is not the learning of facts, it's rather the training of the mind to think."
      – Albert Einstein

My lead engineer, also working second shift at the tunnel, explained the current work assignment to me. The Advanced F-15 group was doing the development work required to incorporate a chin pod on the lower centerline of the forward fuselage, just in front of the nose landing gear. This PSWT wind tunnel test would provide aerodynamic increments for the chin pod, i.e. what influence the chin pod had on basic aircraft stability.

The primary concern with the pod was the added side area located forward on the aircraft and the degrading influence it could have on directional stability. The F-15 had two big vertical tails that provided an adequate level of directional stability (similar to the feathers on the back of an arrow), but adding any side area up front had the equivalent effect of cancelling out or reducing some of the stability provided by the vertical tail area.

So, the question du jour was how *much* of a reduction in stability did the chin pod cause, and would there still be an *adequate* level to perform the required mission?

[Author's note: One paragraph does not fully explain the situation. Not even close. There were a whole host of issues to be considered and resolved, only one of which was directional stability. I had no concept of the magnitude of this task. However, after reading the lone paragraph above, you, the reader, know as much about the situation as I did that day. In pilot speak, I was an empty cluebag.]

Eager to jump in, I offered a heartfelt, "Yes sir, how can I help?" My new lead engineer asked me, "Can you write legibly?" Well, as it just so happened, my penmanship was *impeccable*. Ever since learning to write in all-cap block letters for my high school drafting class, I was a convert. No more of that curlicue fancy cursive writing for me. "Yes," although feeling a bit dejected that *that* was the only thing being asked of me. "Good," he said, then handed me a stack of wind tunnel data plots needing titles written on them.

Writing titles on data plots. For the better part of two weeks. On second shift. My penmanship was so good, in fact, the two aero engineers on first shift took note of it, and saved all of their data plot labeling for me – lucky bastard. It was good to feel wanted, I suppose, even if it had nothing to do with the technical degree earned with so much sweat during the past five years. Had I survived a semester of Heat Transfer *Hell* just to label plots? "Yes," was the answer to that rhetorical question, as a matter of fact. (Heat Transfer *Hell* – that's funny. Get it? ICMU.)

[Author's note: In hindsight, my adding titles to data plots was beneficial to the experienced engineers, as it freed up their time to examine the details of the wind tunnel test results; a fact I did not come to appreciate until later in my career.]

The months following the wind tunnel test were spent writing the test report, creating aerodynamic increments, running six degree of freedom (6-DOF) trajectory predictions, and preparing for flight testing. 6-DOF was a computer simulation program containing math models of the aircraft, including aerodynamics, flight control system, engines, landing gear, etc. Engineers, such as myself, would set up cases to emulate how a pilot would perform certain maneuvers and then run those cases at various flight conditions. It was essentially the same thing as having a pilot fly in the simulator, except we could run it at our desk, and we could run the exact same control inputs each time at each condition. It also allowed us to vary one thing at a time and see the effect.

As each day went by, more and more was learned about just how much I *didn't* know. Every *little* step taken or every *little* thing completed just opened the door for more to do and more to learn. Would I ever get to stop *learning* new stuff and spend more time just *doing* stuff? Kind of like learning to ride a bike, and then spending the rest of your childhood enjoying bike riding. In effect, that day would never come.

ER: Engineers don't solve the *same* problem over and over again. If they did, their job could be done by a trained monkey. Engineers are paid to *think* and solve *new* problems.

After wrapping up the 6-DOF trajectory predictions, the flight testing phase was rapidly approaching. Testing with the chin pod would be done from St. Louis because this was a company funded program, as opposed to a USAF program. One lesson learned during this program was flight testing was expensive. *High speed* flight testing was even more expensive. Approximate numbers of $50,000+ per flight were thrown around. The F-15 carried about 2,000 gallons (14,000 lbs) of fuel internally, most of which would be burned on a mission. Plus each test mission had a few dozen people watching it, if you included all the disciplines like engineering, aircrew, management, maintenance, ground ops, etc. So, you could see that even a relatively short one-hour flight, preceded by a pre-flight briefing and followed by a post-flight briefing, would consume an inordinate amount of fuel and man-hours.

Because flight testing was so expensive, we were allowed to test only that which was absolutely required. For our chin pod program, the primary issue at hand was directional stability at high speeds, or high *Mach number* (see definitions at the back). Thus testing had to focus at high Mach, and that testing had multiple issues associated with it.

One issue was the large amount of airspace required for the jet to operate in while flying fast. It took time (and thus distance) to accelerate out to the test conditions desired (Mach 1.2 to 2.0). The test jet had to stay within radio contact and telemetry range of MDC Flight Ops in St. Louis. Plus it had to operate in the airspace allowed by and coordinated with Air Traffic Control (ATC) at Kansas City Center.

Another issue was the amount of fuel it took just to get to the desired high Mach conditions. The F-15's two engines, while producing a boatload of thrust, also burned about 60,000 to 80,000 lbs of fuel per hour in full afterburner at the conditions we needed to test at. It takes no great mathematician to figure out that burning fuel at that rate, while carrying only 14,000 lbs of total fuel, left precious little fuel/time available after reaching the target test condition. In general, for this kind of testing, by the time the jet takes off, climbs out, and accelerates to the test condition Mach number, there was time for but a scant few maneuvers before the pilot must retard the throttles, slow down and turn for airspace, or declare *bingo* fuel and return to base (RTB).

[Author's note: Bingo fuel is the amount of fuel it is estimated to require to get back to base and land, with some reserves in case an emergency situation develops, or in case the pilot must divert to another field. The pilot determines the bingo fuel level in advance and sets a pointer on the fuel gauge. When the fuel drops to that level, a voice warning sounds, BINGO FUEL.]

More specifically, the F-15 accelerated rather smartly out to Mach 1.6 or so, but above that the acceleration rate slowed noticeably. For example, if the test condition was Mach 2, we would see Mach number slowly creep up on our displays. 1.95... a few seconds elapse, 1.96... a few more seconds, 1.97... etc., until we reached on condition at 2.00 Mach and could begin maneuvering. It was a race to see if the jet could get to the test condition before running out of airspace or running out of fuel. The jet was travelling at 1300 miles per hour and burning 80,000 lbs of fuel per hour. Simple math told us every minute at those conditions used up 22 miles of airspace and 1350 lbs of fuel. It was numerically obvious we did not have an abundance of minutes to play with.

Yet another issue with high speed testing, and the issue having the most impact, was at high airspeeds or Mach numbers there was little to no margin for error. At those speeds, if something went wrong, if the jet yawed too much during a roll (due to not enough directional stability perhaps), it would break apart and disintegrate. The jet would not come back. The pilot would not come back. It would all be over in less than two or three seconds. There would be little warning, and no time for the aircrew to eject. Even if they could eject, doing so at those high speeds came with no guarantees of success or survival. The speeds involved and loads on the airframe were simply too high to tolerate a failure of any kind.

The Advanced F-15 program was in the process of, in the *business* of, adding a chin pod to the jet. The F-15 was (and is) a fighter with Mach 2+ capability. The program decided we had to demonstrate that capability with the new chin pod installed as well. It was settled, we would conduct a flight test program that would prove adequate stability and controllability while maneuvering at speeds up to Mach 2.

No, it was *not* settled. There were ongoing debates on the merits of this testing. Not the kind of debates where engineers sat across a table and discussed the pros and cons of a particular design, but rather the kind of debates among engineers, pilots, and *managers* that discussed risk levels and yes, life and death. I sat in flight test planning meetings, watching and hearing grown men literally *scream* at each other, pound the table, and at times storm out. Our technical integrator (highest ranking engineer on the program) demanded the testing be done because the Flight Manual said the F-15 was a Mach 2+ jet and we had an obligation to prove it. In other words, if we, the contractor, were scared to fly to the limits with a chin pod installed, then how could we release that new capability to a fleet pilot? The chief flight test engineer (highest ranking engineer in the flight test organization) argued back to him something to the effect, "You are not putting *my* pilots and *my* aircraft at risk just because you think the Flight Manual says you can."

It was an eye-opening, jaw-dropping experience for this newb, barely a year out of college. I had no clue why the debate got so heated or why the emotional levels were so charged. I had no clue of the risks (yet). I had no clue of the history (yet). These were decisions that defied simple engineering logic. These were decisions that were going to be made at a level well above my pay grade. I kept my mouth firmly shut – a task immensely easier given I knew nothing and was well aware of the fact I knew nothing.

ER: You may have a thought in your head, but that doesn't mean it has to come out of your mouth.

Or possibly more eloquently;

> "Courage is what it takes to stand up and speak, it's also what it takes to sit down and listen."
> – Winston Churchill

Both sides seemed to have valid arguments. How could a contractor, in good conscience, release a new capability to a fleet pilot, some young lieutenant say, if they were not willing to test it themselves? On the other hand, while the Flight Manual did contain a basic list of airspeed limitations and associated prohibited maneuvers, it was not all-inclusive, and was never meant to be. Pilots learned when and where they could aggressively maneuver the jet, and when not to, regardless if the Flight Manual specifically prohibited it or not. The chief flight test engineer's argument was just because the Flight Manual didn't specifically *prohibit* a pilot from doing a full lateral stick roll at Mach 2, for example, that didn't imply it was *smart* to do a full stick roll at Mach 2. Not only was it considered not a smart thing to do, but it was also not considered an *operationally relevant* maneuver to perform. The number of F-15 pilots who ever reached Mach 2 in their flying careers could probably be counted on one hand, or so the argument went. The number of F-15 pilots who reached Mach 2 *and* did a full stick roll was, well... presumed to be zero. If there was no *tactical* need to do a full stick roll at Mach 2, and no sane pilot would do it, then was it really necessary to put a test pilot and test aircraft at risk just to prove it could be done? Depended on your point of view.

There was also recent history involved. A few years earlier a new production F-15B, flying out of Lambert Airport, was lost while doing a high speed run. Every new production jet coming off the assembly line had to be flown, with a contractor pilot, to approximately Mach 2 to verify all the aircraft systems were working. This particular F-15, after starting its speed run, did not come back. There was no data, as production jets were not instrumented, so it could not be determined with any certainty what the cause was. One could only surmise, I suppose, knowing that the pilot had started his speed run, but having few if any significant pieces of wreckage to examine, that the aircraft had disintegrated up at altitude. This was all too fresh in the minds of the flight test community, as they had lost one of their own at high Mach. They certainly did not want a repeat. Emotions ratcheted up, understandably.

I was not privy to the final discussions on whether to test at high speed or not. After the initial heated exchanges, subsequent meetings were held at high levels only, and behind closed doors. It would've been interesting to have been the proverbial fly on the wall in those meetings, but no matter, I had plenty of other tasks to busy myself with.

Soon the verdict was returned. High speed flight testing would be conducted. We were going to Mach 2. We were going to do full stick rolls. The onus immediately shifted to us, aero engineering, to prove it was safe to do this testing, and to plan out how to conduct the test program in a safe build-up approach.

That safe build-up approach involved three cornerstones. First, testing at lower (but still *supersonic*) Mach numbers would be done prior to testing at higher Mach numbers. Second, benign maneuvers would be performed before attempting more aggressive maneuvers. For example, doublets would be performed before rolls, and *half* lateral stick rolls performed prior to *full* lateral stick rolls. Finally, data from one flight would be analyzed, and 6-DOF predictions updated, prior to proceeding to the next flight. Sounded like a plan.

The problems with a nice, safe build-up approach were *time* and *money*. As spelled out earlier, high speed flight testing was both expensive and time-consuming. The reality of the situation was budgets were not unlimited, and schedules were not open-ended. We simply could not have *every* test point we wanted. We had to pick and choose. We could not spend *weeks* analyzing data after every test flight. We had to compromise. We had to settle for less – less data and less time.

ER: What an engineer *wants*, in terms of test data and time to analyze said data, and what an engineer *gets*, are generally two entirely different things.

After all the test planning and initial 6-DOF predictions were completed, it was time to actually start flying. This was all so brand new to me, having never monitored flight testing before. Eager? Yes. But *comfortable*? No. We decided three aero engineers would monitor the test flights, each sitting in front of a strip chart machine, each machine having eight pens displaying a real-time graph of pertinent data parameters. Each engineer would be assigned one *critical* data parameter to watch intently, and to make *go/no-go* safety calls based on. One of those parameters was mine.

This was heady stuff, as you might imagine. A scant year out of college and my very first flight test assignment. The specific monitoring task given to me was understood, but in all honesty, I didn't have enough experience to even know what I didn't know.

The pressure during a high speed run was intense. There was precious little time to *think*. The combined issues of acceleration time, high fuel burn rates, and limited airspace meant once the jet got on condition, we had to be ready to clear the pilot to maneuver NOW! And once one maneuver was completed, we had to be ready to clear the pilot to the next maneuver NOW! There was no time to discuss the results amongst ourselves until the speed run was over. In fact, there was not even time to speak to the test conductor, so, in lieu of speaking, we devised a scheme where each of the three aero engineers held up one hand continuously – thumbs up if it was OK to proceed, and thumbs down if we had to terminate testing. If the test conductor saw three thumbs up, then it was OK to proceed. Keeping one hand *airborne* left only one hand available to write notes, flip pages, point to prediction values on a page, or key the mike if required. The phrase *busier than a one-armed paper hanger* comes to mind.

In addition to the lack of time available to process information or discuss results, there was that other nagging issue of high speed testing – no margin for error – combined with the recent mishap, which lingered not in the back, but in the *forefront* of our minds. I had eight squiggly pens to watch, and my assigned one parameter to focus on. I had a predicted value for that parameter for every maneuver at every flight condition. It was my job to look at the value of that data parameter, compare it to the predicted value, and decide whether it was safe to proceed to the next, less benign, test point. My thumb's job was to relay that information to the test conductor, who would then relay it to the pilot. If my thumb was wrong, there was a chance the aircraft and the pilot would not come back. Same for the other two engineers. The implications were potentially *that* dire.

Recent history confirmed that. And the visual image of a Roman emperor using his thumb up or down to decide the life or death of a gladiator was not lost on us either.

The problem one quickly learned about flight testing, was that *real* aircraft test conditions or results were neither exact nor consistent. Computer 6-DOF predictions, in contrast, *were* exact and consistent. 6-DOF simulations could be driven with crisp and *perfect* pilot model inputs, e.g. stick input magnitude, duration, etc. Simulations could be initialized at *exact* flight conditions, e.g. Mach, altitude, etc. Maneuver simulations could be run ten times and would get the *same* answer each time. 6-DOF predictions were, in effect, a *sterile* environment. Flight testing was not.

In the process of making our go/no-go calls, it was our job to take *non-sterile* results from the prior maneuver, compare them to the *sterile* 6-DOF predictions sitting in our laps, and make the judgment call whether it was safe to proceed to the next maneuver or flight condition. Oh, and by the way, do it NOW! What if the maneuver was supposed to be half lateral stick, but the pilot put in slightly *less* than half, or slightly *more* than half? What if the bank angle change was supposed to be 180 degrees, but the pilot went past 180? What if the prediction was run at Mach 1.80 but the aircraft was actually at Mach 1.82? What if the pilot put in slightly more than half stick, *and* overshot 180 degrees bank angle, *and* started a bit too fast? These were the situations that had to be dealt with. These were the situations where a newb like myself would've liked to have had prior experience, or be able to discuss the results with his lead engineer.

It is worth noting that in many subsequent flight test programs, we would conduct piloted simulation (*sim* for short) sessions to practice for emergency procedures (EPs) and other possible contingencies. During these sessions we would insert some sort of simulated aircraft failure or degraded mode. The intent was to see if the pilot recognized it, see if the engineers recognized it, and then to rehearse the prescribed recovery procedures and the calls to be made. Some failure scenarios were quick and easy to diagnose and recover from, others were not. We had our share of sim runs that took the jet all the way to ground impact, requiring the pilot to also *simulate* an ejection (because even the final act of ejection required calls to be made).

For this test program, however, there were no EP sim sessions. There was essentially no point practicing for contingencies when there could be no recovery from them. We had go/no-go calls to make, certainly, but those were based on *past* results, to be made *prior* to starting the next maneuver. Once a maneuver was started, there was no going back, no stopping it. The pilot was effectively along for the ride for those few seconds. Think Olympic high diving – once the diver stepped off the platform, he or she was fully committed, and was going to hit the water. For us, if the maneuver went badly, no amount of engineering calls or heroic pilot airmanship was going to stop it. There could be no *miracle on the Hudson* moment.

I'm no expert on space flight, but I think our situation was similar to both the liftoff and reentry phases of Apollo and Space Shuttle missions. Each had scads of engineers monitoring all sorts of parameters. Each had a primary test conductor talking to the astronauts. But once that rocket motor was lit, or once reentry to the atmosphere was initiated, they were committed. The astronauts were along for the ride. The engineers in mission control, in their own way, were just along for the ride. You looked at your charts. You monitored your data. *You did your job.* But in reality, all you could do was hope they came out on the other side intact.

Back to chin pod flight testing...

During one particular high speed run, we did not assess the data and make our calls in time. The prior maneuver's results were borderline. The conditions weren't perfect. We needed just a bit more time to *think.* The test conductor, seeing neither thumbs up nor thumbs down, was insistent, "Can we proceed?" The pilot, hearing nothing from the test conductor, was doubly insistent, "Am I cleared to maneuver?" After a few seconds, a *few too many* seconds as it turned out, the pilot uttered an expletive and said, "OK, we're done, I'm out of airspace." He throttled back and waited to slow down enough to start the turn back to base. The mission was over. There was not enough fuel to accelerate out to high Mach again.

There were a dozen or more people in the control room, each frustrated, each looking at us three engineers. It would now take *another* flight to get these test points done. The mood in the post-flight debrief was a bit down, unsurprisingly. The test pilot was frustrated at not getting the expected *"cleared to maneuver"* call in a timely manner. Also unsurprisingly, I suppose – when you are travelling at over 1300 mph and burning fuel at 80,000 lbs per hour, you tend to want answers NOW. *But we had done our jobs.* If the results were not *as expected*, then it was our job to take the time we needed to be certain before proceeding. The risks were simply too high.

However, there was also the added risk of having to go back up there again to be considered. We were flying in a region of the envelope with no margin for error, neither engineering error nor an aircraft system fault, and it was tempting fate every time we traversed. Limiting exposure to these regions of the envelope was something on the minds of everybody involved. And that's just what we needed, *more* pressure.

ER: Engineers should not request high speed flight testing unless the data to be acquired is deemed an absolute necessity.

During the debriefing, we did our best to explain our situation to the pilot and the test team assembled. The pilot, although again frustrated by the results, fully understood our predicament, and thus our apparent lack of decisiveness. It was, after all, his butt in the seat. Although never spoken, I could only assume he took little comfort knowing that one of the three critical parameters was being monitored by a 23 year old newb engineer, still dripping wet behind the ears.

My First Assignment

This assignment was my first interaction with a pilot other than my father, and my first ever interaction with a *test* pilot. I came away impressed.

Sorry, we've gone way too long without a joke...

Flying: Because soccer, baseball, football, basketball, and golf only require ONE ball.

The chin pod flight test program ended without incident, thankfully. I survived, actually *thrived*, and in the process learned an enormous amount. Trial by fire. It was more than a bit ironic that the chin pod and the sensors it held were never selected by the USAF to be incorporated on the F-15. So, all that development work we did was essentially for naught. But that mattered little to me – I was hooked. F-15 flight testing was going to all but consume my engineering life.

[Author's note: I didn't know it at the time, but this was <u>not</u> the way to conduct a high risk flight test program. A fresh out of college engineer with no experience should never have been thrust into such an intense situation, especially on their very first flight test assignment. The safety of a pilot and aircraft should not have relied upon the calls from an engineer with no prior flight test experience. There were a host of things to be learned about flight testing – the techniques, the environment, the protocol, the subtleties. The time to learn these things was either during a benign test program, or as a non-participant observer watching other engineers do the job. The time was not while doing full stick rolls at Mach 2, where the outcome of a mistake or error in judgment was potentially catastrophic.]

Photo of F-15B#2 (tail number 71-0281) with prototype chin pod installed, circa 1985. Photo credit unknown.

CHAPTER 4
ENGINEER VERSUS PILOT – AN INTRODUCTION

"At that time (1909) the chief engineer was almost always the chief test pilot as well. That had the fortunate result of eliminating poor engineering early in aviation."
  – Igor Sikorsky

That last chapter was kind of a doozie, huh? Didn't the back cover of this book say something about being light-hearted and humorous? A thousand pardons. Let's get that situation rectified shall we...

Most of my work focused on the F-15, which had its first flight in 1972, thus it had been flying long before I started working at MDC. I always wanted to work on aircraft that were already flying because I wanted to work with a *real* product, something tangible, something having *real* takeoffs and *real* landings. I never understood those guys who liked to work on advanced design programs – they were just paper airplanes, the majority of which never won a bid or developed into a real aircraft. I realize *somebody* must do the advanced design work, and more power to them, but it just wasn't my cup of tea – too much of an energy drain to work on something for years but not see anything tangible come from it. But I digress.

Since most of the *new* things I worked on for the F-15 eventually did make it onto the jet, which then had to be flight tested, a lot of time was spent dealing with pilots, both of the military and company/contractor variety. After spending so much time with pilots, I eventually built a rapport with them. Certainly, rapport is one word to describe the relationship. Other words also come to mind; conflict, disgust, resentment; but also envy and respect. For me the word of choice was *banter*.

Not too surprisingly, most of the engineers I worked with tended to put pilots on a pedestal. They had the mindset that if a pilot said something, well then it simply must be true. Huh? I wondered where that came from. Remember my history with my father and his arrogant fighter pilot buddies who basically knew diddly about airplanes? I guess I came into this fight loaded for bear, as it were. It was an almost sense of *duty* to give these guys a healthy dose of crap at every possible opportunity. If my fellow engineers were building pedestals for pilots, it was my job to knock them off every once in a while.

The beauty of this situation was that pilots, most being bullshitters by their very nature, were quite skilled and capable of returning as much as I could dish out. Thus, the back and forth banter between pilots and myself. More examples to follow later. I'm not claiming to have invented the concept of this banter, but I was not going to let it fall by the wayside on my watch either. Respect maybe, but no pedestals here.

I've been using the word *pilot* so far, but to be more technically correct, I should use the word *aircrew*, especially since most of my time was spent working on the F-15E, which is a two-seat aircraft. There are many names for the, ahem, *second* aircrew member. GIB (guy in back) is probably the easiest and most accurate, since the job entails sitting in the back seat, sometimes called the *pit*. The USAF calls the F-15E backseater a WSO (weapon system operator) – pronounced *wiz-oh*, not to be confused with *wiz-urd* by any means. The Navy calls their back seater a RIO (radar intercept officer) or NFO (naval flight officer). Ah, a rose by any other name...

Time for another joke...

> *I've flown in both pilot seats; can someone tell me why the other one is always occupied by an idiot?*

OK, one more, from the WSO perspective...

> *I had always heard that the main function of WSOs was to give the aircraft READ and WRITE capability.*

OK, OK, just one more, I promise...

> *One of the beautiful things about a single piloted aircraft is the quality of the social experience.*

Having an aerodynamics and flight controls background, I concerned myself with how the jet performed and handled. In our world, the discipline was called *Performance and Flying Qualities*, or P&FQ for short. If it was not directly related to how the jet performed and handled, then we P&FQ types tended to lump everything else together under the general heading of *avionics*, which included all manner of ills such as navigation, radios, radar, electronic warfare, counter measures, etc.

Basically, avionics guys are just button pushers and bit twizzlers. The airplane is just something (a platform) to deliver their avionics and/or weapons to a certain point on a map. They don't care how it gets there. In stark contrast, P&FQ types could not care less about pushing buttons and scrolling displays, they want to know *how* the aircraft flies. How quickly and safely can it maneuver? Can it outperform an adversary? What amount of pilot workload is required to accomplish a task? (Not that we engineers truly *care* about how much effort the pilot must exert, but it's a textbook thing to assess handling, thus we feel compelled to check that box. Also, having an engineer *ask* a pilot about his workload after the mission helps perpetuate the illusion that engineers *do* care about pilots. Some egos need to be stroked.)

Back on point though. To an avionics guy, a *maneuver* is something done in between flying straight & level and pushing a button, and is something to be avoided if at all possible. For P&FQ types, the *maneuver* is THE item of interest. All of that 1g straight & level crap is just monotonous drivel filling up our computer buffers. In *Top Gun* speak, *"Come on Maverick, do some of that pilot shit..."*

[Author's note: "g" is a unit of normal acceleration, also called load factor. 1g is what is experienced under normal gravity, say just sitting in your comfy chair. Pilots feel higher than 1g load factors when they pull back on the stick, a term called pulling g's for obvious reasons. Fighter pilots routinely get to feel high g load factors during maneuvering. Test pilots also routinely get to feel high g load factors during maneuvering, all the while being monitored by an audience of engineers, who are stuck sitting in their comfy but boring 1g chairs. Remember the words: disgust, resentment, and envy?]

Back to WSOs. We've established the pilot's primary job is to *fly* the airplane, and the WSOs primary job is to *push* a button. It doesn't take much thought to realize we aero engineer types have little use for WSOs (except at the bar, discussed in a later chapter). This realization leads to an apropos name for the backseater: *ballast*, or more accurately, *missionized* ballast, or even *self-loading* ballast. When you get down to it, when you peel back all the layers, the de facto primary role of the WSO is to help keep the aircraft center of gravity (CG) ahead of the aft limit. And if a sack stuffed with 170 pounds of potatoes strapped into the back seat can do that job just as well as the 50th percentile aviator...

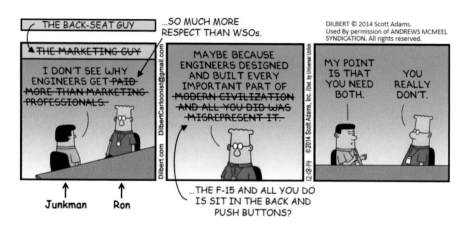

I should go on record here as admitting that yes, the Aerospace industry does indeed need avionics types. I would just prefer it if we could keep them at a distance. I mean, can't they go sit in another building? And I suppose if the industry needs avionics types, then one would have to admit the industry also needs WSOs. Somebody's got to push those buttons while airborne; they won't just push themselves, right? Well, unless someone writes a script to do that, but that's a different story, I suppose. OK, fine, I accept the world needs WSOs too. Happy?

To be honest, a distinction should be made that while a WSO may have only limited usefulness on a *test* mission, that same situation does not apply during actual training or combat. During training and combat the WSO has a plethora of roles to fulfill, and is likely busier than a mosquito at a nudist colony. Plus having that second set of eyes in the cockpit has no doubt saved jets throughout the history of aerial warfare.

And by the way, I've been told being a WSO is a step *above* being a Navigator, so there is also that going for them. But anyway, don't go feeling too bad for WSOs. No need to shed any tears. WSOs, just like pilots, have got this banter thing down pat and are quite adept at slinging it back at *both* engineers and their pilot brethren. In fact, WSOs commonly refer to the front-seat occupants as Random Stick Monkeys (RSM).

Game on.

A bit of background before we continue...

A large portion of this book will be filled with pilot (RSM?) and WSO anecdotes – both the good and the bad. In a feeble attempt to protect any innocence, whether real or perceived, the author shall endeavor to refer to them by their call signs instead of their names.

As a side note, did you ever wonder how fighter pilots got their call signs? Well, per Wikipedia:

> USAF fighter call signs are given at naming ceremonies or "namings". They are usually based on how badly you've screwed something up, a play on your name, your personality, or just the whims of the drunken mob of pilots. Usually once a pilot flies with a call sign in combat they get to keep it for their career.

As a side to this side note, try asking a pilot sometime what his call sign *means*, or how he *earned* it. Experience tells me, about half the time, the only response you will get is some sort of non-verbal grimace. And with that you will know – it was either 1) because of a major embarrassment, or 2) the backstory cannot be spoken in mixed company (remember *drunken mob of pilots*).

OK, back on topic. Below is a story from a guy (call sign *Rabbit*, no idea why) with a unique perspective – he started out as a WSO and then worked as a flight test engineer. Sums it up nicely.

> Having been a proud backseater in the formidable F-4G Wild Weasel I feel I can relate to both sides. Usually we backseaters were included with our nose gunners when the name calling started and whatever they claimed to be true we would swear to as the gospel. And they also would do the same for us. Many a disciplinary action was averted by the testimony of 2 aircrew. (Sir, we were not even close to Death Valley. It had to be a Navy F-4 from China Lake doing strafing passes on those RVs. He's right sir. We weren't within 100 miles of Death Valley.) However, having been out of the cockpit for numerous years and working on the 'other side' I have noticed some aircrew attributes that made me wonder if things are different now. So, I went to the source of all truth. My wife. And, I asked her what I was like back then in a flight suit and if I was different now. Quote "Back then you were a conceited ass with a big watch. Now you're just an ass."
>
> Rabbit

Speaking of wives, here's another joke...
Navigator spouses always ask "How come you're not a WSO?"
WSO spouses always ask "How come you're not a pilot?"
Pilot spouses always ask "How come you're not an astronaut?"
I wonder what astronaut spouses ask about...

And one more joke to finish out the topic of a two-man crew...
Q. What is the ideal cockpit crew?
A. A pilot and a dog. The pilot is there to feed the dog, and the dog is there to bite the pilot in case he tries to touch anything.

One more story about button pushers and bit twizzlers...

I would regularly attend the F-15 Flight Manual Review Conference (FMRC) each year. It's basically a conference room full of pilots, WSOs, and engineers, and our job is to review and accept, reject, or modify recommended changes to the Flight Manual. It's typically three to four days of hashing out wording and syntax on the changes we agree to accept, and for the proposed changes we reject it's figuring out how to tell the person who submitted the proposed change that it's either not required, or sometimes just downright stupid.

The F-15 Flight Manual has eight chapters. One chapter is for aircraft limits – i.e. what a pilot is supposed to do and not do with my jet – pretty good stuff. Another chapter is for emergency procedures – i.e. what happens when a pilot messes with my jet, and how to potentially get themselves out of their self-induced predicament – not bad stuff. Yet another chapter is for flight characteristics – i.e. how my jet flies – which is just friggin' awesome, thank you very much. The remaining five chapters are primarily focused on displays, buttons, and other manners of watching paint dry. So, as might be inferred, much of the FMRC is a waste of time for someone such as myself.

In one particular FMRC, hosted by Robins AFB, there was a discussion about the correct terminology for button pushing and use of the Castle switch (located on the stick and side controllers in the cockpit). Anyway, and no joke, there was a debate on whether it's more correct to say BUTTON – PUSH or BUTTON – DEPRESS. The conference room was full of people, several more had called in from remote locations, and we were spending time trying to decide if a button is *pushed*, or is it *depressed*? In valley girl speak – *OMG*.

Was that enough? No. After the button depress fiasco, we moved on to a topic involving moving the 4-direction Castle switch (it can be toggled forward, back, left, and right). The Castle switch on the side controller in the aft cockpit is oriented almost horizontal, so pushing the switch *forward* sounds correct. But the Castle switch on the center stick is oriented more upright, almost vertical, so pushing the switch *upward* sounds more correct. To be honest, there's no way to screw up the action, whether it's worded as CASTLE – FWD or CASTLE – UP, it'll have the same result. And to be brutally honest, who gives a crap? We spent *four* hours that day discussing whether the Castle switch is moved forward or up. I want those four hours of my life back. Thankfully there was no conceivable way to mix up left vs right, or so you might think, keep reading...

I worked with a pilot, Flood, for years who just could not get the concept of left versus right. If we gave Flood a flight card that directed him to input *left stick* or *left pedal*, we had about a 50% chance he'd follow the card, which is not too bad, I suppose, considering there are only *two* options to choose from. The first couple of times it happened, we engineers thought no big deal, everybody makes a mistake now and again. But after 20 years of mixing up left vs right, it's no infrequent mistake. It's a full-fledged trait. It's part of his Polish Neanderthal DNA. It's actually something to *count on* occurring. Better hope no maneuvers are planned where putting the stick one direction is benign but putting it the other is potentially dangerous. If so, save that test card for another pilot...

I don't want to be too harsh. Everybody has their flaws. Remember I can type the letter *x* with only a 75% chance of success.

It took a while to reach this conclusion, but am now convinced it was not a trait, not part of his DNA, but rather he did this *intentionally* to yank my chain. When it came to setting up strip charts for monitoring test flights, I was anal-retentive. Each parameter was oriented to move in the same direction the jet was going, if at all possible. For example, for a roll to the right, the roll rate and bank angle pens on the strip chart would move to the right, regardless of which direction was a positive or negative numerical value. You knew, at a glance, whether the jet was moving the direction expected – one could figure out the positives/negatives and magnitudes when there was time.

Here's how a typical maneuver might have gone. The card directed the pilot to input *Full Left Stick*. This was what the test plan said. This was what was practiced in the simulator. This was what we engineers had predictions for. This was what was briefed at the pre-mission briefing. Just prior to the performing the maneuver the test conductor called to the pilot – "*OK, next maneuver is Full Left Stick*". WSO (who has nothing to do but read the upcoming test cards) echoed – "*Full Left Stick.*" Flood confirmed – "*Full Left Stick.*"

And then, as if out of nowhere, Flood inserted full *right* stick. I stared at my strip charts. The jet was *not* responding properly. Did I call *Recover*, or *Terminate*, or *Knock It Off* (any of which would've been appropriate given the lack of proper aircraft response)? No. I calmly reminded myself that Flood was the pilot. I did what I've done for 20 years – sighed and called "*good maneuver*". The test conductor hesitated for a moment, then parroted – "*good maneuver*". Flood responded – "*Roger, good maneuver*", no doubt satisfied my chain has been sufficiently yanked. WSO remained silent. Sack of potatoes silent.

I don't say this publicly often, but I secretly hope there is a special place in Hell for pilots who like to torment engineers. Likewise, I assume there will also be a special place in Hell for engineers who like to torment pilots, and if so, then I'm fairly certain to have a reserved seat waiting for me. I just pray those two *special* places are not one and the same. Spending an eternity in Hell is something I can accept as my fate. Spending an eternity in Hell in the company of pilots would be borderline unbearable.

↑ Manager   ↑ Ron

Photo of the author (right) and test pilot Flood (left) in front of F-15E#1 at Edwards AFB, circa 1994. Note the devilishly good looks, the steely eyes, and the charismatic smile. Flood is not too bad looking either, I suppose. Photo credit unknown.

CHAPTER 5
TEST PILOTS VERSUS MERE MORTAL PILOTS

As if my work wasn't harmonious enough having to deal with pilots and WSOs. No, I had to work with *test* pilots and *test* WSOs. Most military and commercial pilots, ahem *aircrew*, are required to have a college degree, but that degree does not have to be technical. Thus, the captain on your international 747 flight or the major flying combat patrol missions could just as easily have been poetry majors in college as anything else. Not true for test pilots. Test pilots must have a technical degree and then typically attend either the USAF or USN Test Pilot School (TPS) during their military stint. Most civilian test pilots I know came from the military, so I'm not aware of a strictly civilian path to become a test pilot, although it may exist.

Test pilots who think they are engineers – aww, how cute is that?

Two types of test pilots exist. One type is the guy who earned an engineering degree from college, but then used said degree as a stepping stone to get a pilot training slot and later transitioned to being a test pilot. The other type is the guy who probably had a similar career path, but instead constantly wielded that engineering degree like a weapon to all of those around him. They talked to us lowly engineers with the underlying tone of *you're just an engineer, but I am an engineer AND a pilot.* The implication was they knew everything there was to know about my job AND how to fly the jet too. Goes without saying, but I much preferred the former over the latter.

The following cartoon captures this pretty well. In all fairness, Flood is not that type of test pilot, but he does like pointing out that he is taller than me. That's not saying very much, but whatever makes him happy...

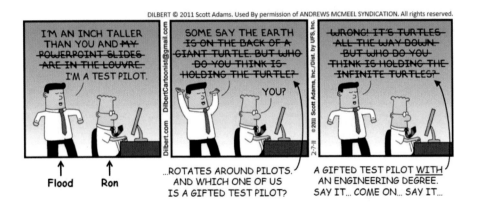

The good news, if you can call it that, is only a few test pilots whom I dealt with fit into the latter category. For me, that meant three of this type. Come to think of it, two of those were ex-Marine Corps pilots. Hmm... More to follow.

Come on test pilot dudes, you simply cannot know everything about everything on your aircraft. I really, really hate to use this phrase, but well... it takes a village. The best test pilots have had one common trait – they know what they know, they know what they don't know, and they embrace and surround themselves with the engineers who know the specialized details they cannot help to know. Sorry, *two* common traits. They also have the gift of banter.

Time for another pilot joke...
   It's not that all airplane pilots are good-looking. It's just that good-looking people seem more capable of flying airplanes.

Here's one I've personally not seen, but was told resides on a plaque in the Test Ops building at Edwards AFB...
   I'm a test pilot. Just because I've never done it before doesn't mean I'm not good at it.

You might surmise, based on reading so far, that I have a certain dislike of test pilots and/or WSOs – that would be entirely wrong. I like them. I like them a lot. Sometimes they just make themselves easy targets for engineers of superior knowledge and intellect, and Air Force bases and flight test assignments are such a target-rich environment. Subtle and good-natured ribbing is par for the course, but sometimes I can get a bit more pointed in nature. Sorry about that. As mentioned previously, I will likely pay for this mightily in the after-life.

[Author's note: To the best of my knowledge, I've never actually been to Hell or ever met Satan. But my fear (recurring nightmare) is that Hell is almost entirely populated by ex-engineers, and Satan and his goons are all ex-pilots. And if spending an eternity in Hell in the company of pilots would be borderline unbearable, then spending an eternity in Hell in the company of test pilots would be... well, it'd be Hell.]

Below is an email exchange I had with one of our test pilots, Dragon, on the subject of pilots.

Subject: a little whine with your crackers...

My Dad celebrated his 80th birthday this week and his kids gave him a surprise party. Anyway, we spent quite a bit of time reminiscing about his time in the USAF – he flew F-86s, F-102s, and F-100s. He was telling us one story when he was flying F-102s out of Paine Field, Wash. Once he had to go to Canada to bring an F-102 back to Washington, and he was complaining about how bitter cold it was doing the pre-flight and sitting in the cockpit waiting for engine start...

I stopped him right there and said "Really? You get to fly faster, higher, and further in one flight than any of us normal people will do in a life-time, and you complain because it's too cold?" I certainly could've stopped there, but no, not me. I went on to generalize this whining must be a fighter pilot thing – as our test pilots are also quick to whine about a host of things, like having to repeat test points for maneuver tolerances for example.

Later that evening at a restaurant for dinner, my Dad whined to the server because they didn't have those little oyster crackers to put in his soup.

Geez. Fighter pilots...

Ron

Subject: RE: a little whine with your crackers...

Bear in mind first and foremost that pilots are NOT whiners. They just happen to be right... about everything. So, what appears to be whining is merely a statement of fact regarding the way life is. It may appear to be whining when viewed by a population that is the most wrong about anything they've ever made a statement about – engineers.

Muse on this: engineers generally state things in terms of a hypothesis; in other words, they state things tentatively, leaving a door open that they might be wrong (which they often are). Hypothesis (along with all engineering) seems to change all the time. Forever new theories, new hypothesis, new testing, things falling off aircraft, new problem reports, request for (yet more) gear down aero data, more misgivings about transonic aero affects, more rolls with less fore or aft stick, more build up plans, more safety chase, more TSMs; the list is endless (and I mean ENDLESS). Money is not the root of all evil - engineering is.

Look at the long trek of scientific/engineering endeavor that finally led to the realization that the world was round. And orbited the sun. Thousands of years of misguided engineering speculation. The aqueducts? Mostly rubble. Pyramids? Tourist attraction. Hanging gardens of Babylon? Myth. Alchemists turning lead into gold? Crackpots. Sadly, as the list is populated, it doesn't look good for engineers.

42

On the other hand, pilots are very positive about what is true. Ever heard "watch this?" We make it happen or die trying. "I've got fuel for one more run?" We get the run or discover an issue with the fuel system that needs to be fixed. "Nothing bad has ever happened there?" We'll prove it to you or exhibit extreme skill recovering from some engineering screw-up.

In the pilot world, we're just right. If it's cold, that's a fact. You can go to the bank with it. It's friggin' cold and we'll tell you. If there are no oyster crackers with our soup, there should have been, and that's a fact. No need for a coat to stay warm, no substitutions of saltines when only oyster crackers will do.

Engineers compromise. Pilots are right. End of story.

Cheers,
Dragon

Did I mention the company promoted Dragon to a *manager*?

43

Snidely   Dragon

Dragon   Flood, Bull, Junkman, Snidely, Peedawg, Phat...

Dragon Flood Snidely

I'm so sorry, Dragon. I really am. But these cartoons... it's almost like they write themselves.

If you're a pilot, a test pilot, or a WSO, and you're struggling with why an engineer, such as myself, would want to dedicate so much time and energy to giving you grief, then maybe this will help. In the book *Consider the Lobster*, the author, David Foster Wallace, talks about himself and other media folks who followed the late Senator John McCain on his 2000 presidential campaign tour. Here is an excerpt.

"One reason a lot of the media on the Trail like John McCain is simply that he's a cool guy... At 63, he's witty, and smart, and he'll make fun of himself and his wife and staff... and he'll tease the press and give them shit in a way they don't ever mind because it's the sort of shit that makes you feel that here's this very cool, important guy who's noticing you and liking you enough to give you shit."

So, there you go, Dragon. The truth is out. I like you enough to give you shit. You can thank me later. And if I'm very cool and important, like John McCain was, well then so much the better for you, I suppose.

And just so you know, Dragon. These things engineers have done: give you grief, modify Dilbert cartoons, and point out your deficiencies in mass distribution emails – well... let's just say it was no walk in the park for us. To take a quote from JFK, we do these things "not because they are easy, but because they are hard."

Time for an engineer joke...

Engineer /en-juh-neer/ noun. Someone who does precision guesswork based on unreliable data provided by those of questionable knowledge. See also wizard, magician.

CHAPTER 6
NOT ALL TEST PILOTS ARE THE SAME

Some background first...

It takes a lot to fly a maneuver on a test mission these days. The glory days back in the 1950s and 60s, when test pilots would just hop in the jet and go try stuff, are long gone. If you are interested in a good book about those days, pick up *Flight Testing at Edwards: Flight Test Engineers' Stories 1946-1975* by Stoliker, Hoey, and Armstrong. It's a different world today.

These days, each test point we want flown has a mountain of paperwork behind it. For the USAF, flight test plans, which include all of the specific test points, maneuver descriptions, flight conditions, background information, etc. are written in a document called a Test Information Sheet (TIS). The US Navy has a similar document, but it is called a Test Working Document (TWD).

Flight test engineers, along with the specific technology engineers (like myself), typically write the TIS with inputs from aircrew. After what can be a lengthy review process, the TIS is approved by engineering, aircrew, and program management. After the TIS is complete, it goes through another process involving a Technical Review Board (TRB), followed by a Safety Review Board (SRB). It is not uncommon for this process to take a year or more from start to finish. TIS writing and review made up a considerable portion of my adult life – not something to brag about for sure.

Another side story...

I was working with one of the flight test engineers, we'll call him Eddie, on several of the TISs for the F-15SA (Saudi) test program. We were absolutely swamped with work, and were having a hard time getting the TIS inputs done when the flight test guys wanted them. During one of our multiple email exchanges, Eddie made a comment about how late the technology engineers (including myself) were with TIS inputs. While true, I felt compelled to respond. So, I replied to Eddie using a parody of the movie *A Few Good Men*:

> You have to ask me nicely. You see, ~~Danny~~ Eddie, I can deal with the bullets and the bombs and the blood, *and program management*. I don't want money and I don't want medals. What I do want is for you to stand there in that ~~faggoty white uniform~~ *tie-dyed T-shirt* and with your ~~Harvard~~ *Rolla* mouth extend me some friggin' courtesy! You gotta ask me <u>nicely</u> *if you want your TIS inputs on time.*

Soon followed by this one...

You can't handle the truth! ~~Son~~ *Eddie,* we live in a world that has ~~walls~~ *airplanes,* and those ~~walls~~ *airplanes* have to be ~~guarded by men with guns~~ *have 6-DOF models.* Who's gonna do it? You? You, ~~Lieutenant Weinberg~~ *Eddie?* I have a greater responsibility than you can possibly fathom. You weep for ~~Santiago~~ *Flight Ops* and you curse the ~~Marines~~ *Technology engineers.* You have that luxury. You have the luxury of not knowing what I know, that ~~Santiago's death~~ *being 6 months late on TIS inputs,* while tragic, probably saved lives. And my existence, while grotesque and incomprehensible to you, saves lives! You don't want the truth, because deep down in places you don't talk about at parties, you <u>want</u> me ~~on that wall~~ *running 6-DOF.* You <u>need</u> me ~~on that wall~~ *running 6-DOF.* We use words like "honor", "code", "loyalty." We use these words as the backbone of a life spent ~~defending~~ *analyzing* something. You use them as a punch line. I have neither the time nor the inclination to explain myself to a man who rises and sleeps under the blanket of the very freedom that I provide, and then questions the manner in which I provide it! I would rather you just said "thank you", and went on your way. Otherwise, I suggest you pick up a ~~weapon~~ *computer,* and ~~stand a post~~ *run some trajectories.* Either way, I don't give a damn what you think you are entitled to!

Did Eddie quit bugging us for TIS inputs? No. Did Eddie get his TIS inputs on time? No. Status quo. Nothing ever changes. So, you might as well have some fun in the process. Eddie was a Rolla grad as well. Not sure what he thought about the bathrooms.

OK, back to the story. We were preparing to flight test a new installation of an Infrared Search & Track (IRST) pod on the F-15E. One of the potential issues of this installation was a reduction in directional stability at high Mach number due to the size and shape of the pod and where it was physically located on the jet (same issue as the chin pod years before). One of the test points needed was to accelerate to Mach 1.8, turn the Control Augmentation System (CAS) off, and perform a set of control stick and rudder pedal doublet inputs. These maneuvers were needed to provide transient response data that would be used to verify and/or update the aerodynamic influence of the IRST installation. I mean, simple stuff, right? It's not like I was asking for a full stick roll.

We sat in the pre-flight briefing to step through the test cards. Dragon was the pilot. We got to the test card with that *Mach 1.8 turn the CAS off thingy,* and the briefing came to a screeching halt. Conversation went something like this:

Dragon: What? You want me to go to Mach 1.8 and turn the CAS off?
Ron: Yes, Dragon.
Dragon: And then you want me to step on the rudder pedal?
Ron: Yes.
Dragon: At that speed?
Ron: Yes.
Dragon: Are you shitting me?
Ron: No.
(pause)

| Dragon: | You do realize that turning the CAS off above Mach 1 is prohibited by the Flight Manual? |
| Ron: | Yes, Dragon. We asked for and received a specific waiver to do these test points. In the past we have done CAS off doublets out to Mach 2. |

(pause)

| Dragon: | OK then, I guess I'm turning the CAS off at Mach 1.8 and giving you a rudder doublet. |
| Ron: | Thank you sir. Much appreciated. |

(pause)

| Dragon: | But you're *not* getting any repeats. (Test pilots *must* have the last word.) |
| Ron: | Understood. (This is a passive response, so technically *not* the last word.) |

[Author's note: Please note the author's tone during the brief exchange of words – calm, cool, and collected in the face of intense pressure and scrutiny, with just a hint of indignation. It's an engineer thing – you may not understand.]

Here's an appropriate gem, credited to *SR-71 Blackbird* author Paul F. Crickmore, *"You've never been lost until you've been lost at Mach 3."* For Dragon, apparently, this occurs at Mach 1.8...

You might wonder why we were having this discussion just minutes *before* the aircrew would step to the jet and fly the mission. Ahh Dragon. Were these test points included in the TIS? Yes. Did aircrew sign off on the TIS? Yes. Were these test points reviewed during the TRB/SRB process? Yes. Did Dragon read the TIS? Well... that may depend on what his definition of *read* was...

In the end, Dragon performed the test points flawlessly and we got the data we needed to verify/update the aerodynamic model. So, it's just one of those things we learned about in dealing with Dragon. He won't read the TIS we wrote (ahh hell, most times he won't even read the Flight Manual), he will wait until the last possible moment to question our test points, but in the end he will capitulate and fly our test points.

In contrast, here's how two of our other test pilots would've likely handled the test.

Flood tended to unleash his criticisms early in the process, during the TIS writing phase. He would spare no red ink marking up our draft TIS editions, and would question every test point, every test condition, every maneuver input – even if they were test points that had been flown since the dawn of jet fuel. But hey, at least it meant he actually read the TIS, so there's a positive difference, I suppose. Once we got past the TIS approval phase, Flood mellowed out considerably and would actively participate in and support us during the TRB/SRB phase. When it came time to fly the test points, there would be no questions and little to no drama.

[Author's note: You might wonder why we didn't have Flood fly the IRST test points, especially since he was the usual flying qualities test pilot, whereas Dragon was typically the avionics test pilot. Well, it's because Flood has a hard time reaching the rudder pedals and we needed a lot of rudder pedal doublets – ha.]

Bull was easy. Bull wouldn't read the TIS. Bull wouldn't participate in the TRB/SRB review. Bull wouldn't question test points during the pre-flight briefing. Bull would perform the test points exactly as prescribed on the test card. No questions. No drama. None. Bull was the anti-Dragon, the anti-Flood.

The bad side of working with Bull was when we happened to need pilot comments and/or ratings to go along with the maneuvers flown. Sometimes engineers just need the recorded aircraft motion data to do our analysis – a blissful state of euphoria, characterized by *more* interaction with numerical data and *less* interaction with emotional people. Sometimes, however, we engineers ask the pilot to do a certain maneuver or task, and we need said pilot to make an assessment of the relative ease or difficulty of performing said task. With Bull, being a man of few words, a typical post-flight briefing would go something like this:

Ron: What was the response of the jet like during this maneuver?
Bull: Fine.
Ron: Fine?
Bull: Yes.
Ron: Would you say the aircraft response was crisp or sluggish?
Bull: No, it was fine.
Ron: Was the response better here compared to the response at say slower or faster speeds?
Bull: Umm... No.
(pause)

Ron: Do you have anything else to add? Any other comments?
Bull: No.
Ron: Really?
Bull: No.
(pause)

Ron: In the near future we will have to write words for the Flight Manual describing the response characteristics of the aircraft during these kinds of maneuvers.
Bull: It was fine.
Ron: I don't think you will find the words "It was fine" anywhere in the Flight Manual.
(awkward silence)

Ron: OK, if you had to brief some new F-15 pilot, some young lieutenant say, who was about to perform this maneuver for the very first time, how would you tell him the jet responds?
Bull: Fine.

[Author's note: Please note the pilot's tone during the brief exchange of words – calm, cool, and collected in the face of intense pressure and scrutiny, with just a hint of indignation. He thinks it's a pilot thing – and it is NOT funny.]

CHAPTER 7
NOT ALL TEST PILOTS ARE THE SAME – PART DEUX

"To the optimist the glass is half full. To the pessimist the glass is half empty. To the engineer the glass is twice as big as it needs to be." – Unknown.

I had another experience further highlighting the differences in test pilots, while working on the Ground Collision Warning System (GCWS) algorithm design for the F-15E in the early 1990s. Once we had a functional design it was time to go to the simulator and have a bunch of pilots evaluate it.

But first a quick side story...

The F-15 has a multitude of voice warnings, in addition to the normal warning tones, beeps, etc. One example is, if the left engine is on fire, the pilot gets a voice warning saying, "*ENGINE FIRE LEFT, ENGINE FIRE LEFT.*" A voice warning is really supposed to get the pilot's attention, as opposed to the myriad of tones and beeps that may possibly go unnoticed during typical maneuvering. When McDonnell Douglas was designing the F-15, they used actual voice recordings (not computer generated) on the aircraft, and the woman who recorded those warnings was named Betty. Since the voice warnings were hard to ignore, the pilots started saying things like, "Yeah, Betty was bitching at me." The name stuck. From that point on the voice warnings were forever referred to as *Bitchin' Betty*.

The GCWS system also had a voice warning, *PULL UP, PULL UP*. During the early sim sessions, since we didn't have the real voice warning system like that installed on the jet, we had to use our own recorded voice warning. And our GCWS sim engineer, Alice, made the recording for us. From that point on her name was *Bitchin' Alice*.

ER: Sometimes, when your boss asks you to do something, you should just politely say no.

Anyway, back to the GCWS sim evaluation. We had to have a *bunch* of pilots evaluate the system because this was going to be one of those designs *nobody* liked, but all for different reasons. When developing a warning system that tells pilots when they are about to hit the ground, we were destined to get some pilots who said it came on too early, some pilots who said it came on too late, and some who simply did not want yet another warning system on their jet. We cannot win. Nobody wins. We ended up with a compromise solution everybody hated, just at varying degrees. And yours truly, as the engineer responsible for conducting the simulator evaluations, bore the brunt of the hateful comments.

GCWS Design   Ron

R2LB: Everything should be made as simple as possible, but no simpler.

Back to the differences between pilots. I told the first pilot in the sim I would like him to fly low enough to the ground to potentially trigger some warnings and evaluate whether or not he thought the warnings were appropriate. No specific maneuvers or flight conditions were specified, just wanted him to do that *pilot stuff* and tell me what he thought. Well, he was having none of that. He wanted specifics. He needed specifics. Essentially, he wanted to be led by the hand through specific conditions. I was unprepared to say the least.

R2LB: There is absolutely no substitute for a genuine lack of preparation.

One specific GCWS thing evaluated was the absolute minimum height above the ground the pilot should get a warning, regardless of airspeed, sink rate, etc. This height was referred to as the Minimum Design Altitude (MDA), because anything of importance in the Aerospace industry simply must have an acronym. Anyway, the initial thought, based on other aircraft designs, was to use 70 feet as the MDA. Well, sim pilot number one thought this was asinine. Nobody in their right mind would fly a multi-million dollar jet that close to the ground on purpose. The MDA needed to be at *least* 100 feet, and for emphasis added the proclamation, "No pilot would ever accept a *lower* altitude."

Having learned my lesson about preparedness, a very detailed set of test cards were in my hands before the next sim evaluation. As a matter of fact, they were just like the ones we used during actual flight testing. So, there we were, myself and Bitchin' Alice, multiple copies of said test cards in hand, and sim pilot number two showed up. I handed him the deck of cards and started walking through them. He stopped me after the second card and said, "That's all well and good, but *this* is what I'm going to do to evaluate your system." With some mild disgust, he handed the test cards back to me, climbed into the simulator cockpit, and proceeded to do whatever he wanted for about 45 minutes. He climbed out of the cockpit and proceeded to tell me how deficient my system was and how no pilot would ever allow it to be installed on his aircraft. He too thought the 70 foot MDA warning was asinine. "When I was a Marine pilot I would spend all day *below* 50 feet," and for emphasis added the proclamation, "No pilot would ever accept a *higher* altitude." Wait a minute. *Higher* altitude? Huh?

"A common mistake that people make when trying to design something completely foolproof is to underestimate the ingenuity of complete fools." – Douglas Adams

Rattled and clueless how to continue with the sim evaluations – I was like the proverbial lab rat who pressed the bar once and got a pellet of food, but pressed the bar again and got an electric shock. Bitchin' Alice was equally perplexed.

In spite of my previous electric shock therapy sessions, there we were again the next morning, your ever dutiful engineering staff, waiting for sim pilot number three. Not knowing if it was right or wrong, I handed him the deck of cards and started walking him through them. Déjà vu. He stopped me after two cards and told me what *he* would do to evaluate the system. But at least he *kept* his copy of the test cards with him. A small victory in my mind. About an hour later I learned *why* he kept his copy – because he didn't have a pad of paper with him and needed the blank backsides of the cards to write his notes on. Yes, another ex-Marine pilot. We'll call him ex-MP2. And yes, I had to endure another "we Marine pilots fly at tree-top level all day long" speech. Spare me. Marine pilots. Sheesh, get over yourselves.

ER: If you design a system. And you like your design. And the users (pilots) like the design. Then you obviously haven't had enough users (pilots) try it.

ER: If you have a sample size of *n* pilots, you will get *n+1* opinions.

I had multiple opportunities to work with ex-MP2 over the years, and many times we were both at Edwards AFB at the same time. On one particular day he asked me if I'd like to join him for lunch at the Officer's Club. Umm. Sure? So, off we go in his rental car. We're driving up a gradual hill along a fairly deserted section of road in the... well... desert. At the crest of the hill, ex-MP2 abruptly takes his foot off the gas and absolutely *jams* the brake pedal to the floor. I lurch forward. I'm no dead language expert here but I think the Latin term is *deceleratus abruptus*. The only thing that keeps me from face-planting on the dashboard is the fact that my seatbelt had a shoulder strap with a functioning inertia reel. Other than shock, the only injuries sustained were contusions to the scapular muscles. Sorry, no twenty-dollar words. My shoulder was bruised.

Ex-MP2 is sitting over there with a grin on his face. Grinning? Really? He turned to me and says, "Yeah, just wanted to check the ABS brakes on the rental." Huh? Why? And even if, how about a little advanced warning maybe? Test pilots. Sheesh. Ex-Marine test pilots. Double sheesh.

The remainder of the car ride was thankfully uneventful, but I was certainly on edge, secretly hoping and praying ex-MP2 wasn't looking for an opportunity to test out the airbags. Remember that special place in Hell reserved for pilots who torment engineers? The front row is reserved for ex-Marine pilots.

R2LB: If you think there is good in everybody, you haven't met everybody.

Many years later I would be re-haunted by this experience. A friend and I were driving back from Ohio on the interstate I-70. It was around dusk. Travelling about 70 mph, we were coming up on an overpass. Just as we crested the hill they came into view – four deer standing on the right shoulder, in the small area between the right lane and the guard rail. Deer *on* the overpass? Nothing could be done. Too late to slow down. Couldn't swerve left because of another vehicle in that lane. Pure instincts. We tensed up and braced ourselves. If the deer spooked and bolted, they had no place to go except *into* our lane, as the other direction would have been over the guard rail and off the side of the overpass to the lanes below. Minds raced with visions of screeching brakes/tires, deer hitting the front bumper, and carcasses crashing into the windshield.

Luckily the deer stood firm and we passed by unscathed. And what popped into my mind just as we passed those deer? Yep, visions of ex-MP2 grinning at me.

Seems quite appropriate to end this chapter with this joke...

It is absolutely imperative that the pilot be unpredictable. Rebelliousness is very predictable. In the end, conforming almost all the time is the best way to be unpredictable.

CHAPTER 8
LIFE IN THE DESERT

"The most important thing is to keep the most important thing the most important thing."
– Donald P. Coduto

I spent a lot of time in the desert. Between all of the flight test assignments, the short term trips, the long term trips, and the pack up the house and move trips, yes I spent a lot of time in the desert. The *high* desert of Southern California (SoCal) to be more specific, also known as the Antelope Valley. It's an area about 70 miles northeast of Los Angeles (LA) encompassing the towns of Palmdale, Lancaster, Rosamond, and Edwards AFB along with the surrounding dry lake beds.

My first trip to Edwards was in June of 1988 to cover the early F-15E flight testing activities. Wedding vows were taken in late May of that same year. So, not long after getting hitched I'm on a plane to LA to spend three months in the high desert. At the time my wife was also working at McDonnell Douglas – her program was the A-6 simulator trainer for the Navy, located at NAS Oceana in Virginia Beach, VA. She also had to travel for work. It just so happened, not long after I returned from my first three month stint at Edwards, she had to leave for a several month stint at Oceana. About the time she got back it was my time to do another stint at Edwards. And thus we alternated. During our first year of marriage we spent less than half of the time together. We jokingly said we had heard the first year of marriage was the most difficult, so we opted to spend it apart.

On my first flight to LA I was a bit taken aback by all the *brown* seen while flying over the country. Once you get about halfway through the state of Kansas, the country turns to *brown*. Consistent and constant *brown*. Basically the entire southwest quarter of the continental US is dirt and sand. After landing in LA, you might see some localized spots of green, but mostly concrete and more *brown*. Then you drive your rental car north over the pass to the Antelope Valley and everything is *brown* again, the color of sand. Dirt and sand. As far as the eye can see.

And to make matters worse, all of the houses and apartment complexes are typically the color of sand. Why? In the Midwest you find houses of all sorts of colors, using paint, brick, or siding. But in the Southwest, everybody uses the color of sand. I need to be educated on this.

I don't know this for a fact, but it's my guess California probably has more grains of sand than any other state in the union. If one counts it on a per capita basis, my guess is Nevada or New Mexico might have the distinction of most grains of sand *per person*. Somebody should do a study on this. Inquiring minds want to know.

After my first three months at Edwards (living in Lancaster), the one thing I missed most of all was seeing *green*. Like I mentioned before, I grew up in the Midwest. I'm a product of the Midwest. I actually *like* the Midwest. It has seasons. The leaves are *green*.

And then they are vibrant reds, yellows, and oranges. And then they fall. Things change. What a concept. It is decidedly *not* the desert.

For example, if you were to hike a trail in Missouri four times in the year, it would likely look different each time. The colors of grasses and leaves. The level of the water in the creek. The moistness or dryness of the soil. The humidity in the air. The wildlife you might see. They all change with the seasons. Not so much in the desert. If you see a patch of dirt in Missouri in the spring, you will likely not find that same patch in the summer or fall. In the desert, that patch of dirt or sand you see has been there, just as it appears, for hundreds of years, and will likely be the same for another hundred years.

During one of my first free weekends at Edwards, a Saturday hike was on the docket. Saddleback Butte State Park peaked my interest, being well within an easy drive of Lancaster. Because of my Midwest upbringing, something on a map labelled state or national forest, or park, or wildlife area, actually meant there was something there worth seeing. A *destination*. Expectations of Saddleback Butte were no less.

After a 30 minute or so drive through the non-descript, featureless desert – arrival. The label on the map said *park*, but this was decidedly not a *park*, not a *destination*. In effect, the state of California put a barbed wire fence around a piece of the desert and declared it a park. Yes, there was the butte to hike up to in the distance, but other than that, the dirt and sand *inside* the fence looked exactly like the dirt and sand *outside* the fence. And if it's just dirt and sand, why the need for a barbed wire fence at all? Is there something unique or special about *my* dirt and sand versus *their* dirt and sand?

Although dejected, the butte itself now became the *destination*, thinking for certain the view from the top had to be scenic – I mean this was a state *park*, wasn't it? About an hour trekking in the direct sun (shade in the desert is as scarce as teeth on a hen) delivered me to the *saddle* portion of Saddleback Butte. The view on the other side of the butte was *amazing*. As in amazingly *exactly* the same as the view on the side I had just trekked. Same non-descript, featureless desert. What a disappointment. And who's at fault? How did I not know, after having just flown over that portion of the country, that it would be the same for hundreds and hundreds of miles? Shame on me.

Speaking of disappointment... At one point during the F-15E development testing, we found ourselves one or maybe two flights short of finishing a particular loading from a flying qualities perspective. The flights were put on the schedule at the F-15 Combined Test Force (CTF) and I found myself on a plane to LA to cover the one or two flights. Short trip. Best case was done in one day. Possibly two days. Worst case was three days. I packed clothes for three days – a Boy Scout is *prepared*. I returned home 28 days later.

Day in and day out we were ready to go. But each day the flight got cancelled, and for a multitude of reasons. My wife kept thinking I would be coming home *tomorrow*. But for almost a month, *tomorrow* never came. After about a week of nightly phone calls explaining why we cancelled the flight for that day, and why I wouldn't be coming home, she got fed up and told me not to call until I knew for certain I was, in fact, returning home. Apparently, no news was better than disappointing news.

Like I mentioned, flights were cancelled for a myriad of reasons – some reasonable and some not so reasonable. The most asinine cancellation was because of the lack of an emblem painted on the side of the vertical tails. Not long before, the base commander issued the decree that all Edwards based test jets should have the new Air Force Materiel Command (AFMC) patch painted on the vertical tails.

The two F-15Es at Edwards were on the list to get painted, but it just hadn't happened yet. Those two jets were in extremely high demand, trying desperately to get operational capability to the then new F-15E fleet, which at the time was deployed in support of the first Gulf War. Painting an emblem on a tail versus flying a mission to support the war was not even a question debated at the F-15 CTF.

Relieved. I am *finally* going to get my flight off. We briefed the mission. Aircrew stepped to the jet, F-15E#2. Engines started up. Instrumentation up and running. All going as planned. The jet taxied out. On the way to the runway the jet passed the Base Ops building. The base commander saw E#2 taxi past, and noticed it did *not* have the now-required AFMC patch painted on the tails. He called the F-15 CTF and ordered the flight cancelled until the tails were painted. E#2 taxied back to the CTF. Livid did not do it justice. The USAF had been known to do stupid stuff on occasion, but this absolutely took the cake. Guess who declined to call his wife and tell her he wasn't coming home for want of a patch?

ER: The USAF is an organization that makes literally thousands of decisions each and every day. There is no hard requirement that those decisions make sense. Logic is not a requirement. On some days it seems like brains are optional...

Photo of F-15E#2 (tail number 86-0184) during an Open House at Edwards AFB, circa 2000. Note extended speedbrake. Note also the AFMC patch on the vertical tail, just above the ED base designation letters – an important patch. Photo credit Peter Davis.

Sports in the desert...

Another disappointment about living in the high desert of SoCal was all the TV coverage originated from LA. Well, that was fine if you were say a Kings fan, a Dodgers fan, or a Raiders fan. No. No. And no. St. Louis Blues fan? KC Royals fan? KC Chiefs fan? Yes. Yes. And most assuredly yes.

With the LA-based TV coverage there were only *two* times you could see the Chiefs play: if they were on Monday Night Football (which didn't happen much), or if the Raiders were playing the Chiefs in KC (when they played in LA it would be blacked out to the local area). I was a junkie. I needed fixes. Twice was not enough, not even close. So, I did what every self-respecting Chiefs fan does when presented with this dilemma – I went to a sports bar to watch the games on the big screen.

Because of the time zone, your standard noon kickoff game started at 10 AM out in LA. So, who could be found, in an empty bar, wearing a Chiefs jersey, at 10 AM on a Sunday morning, alone? I'm fairly certain it was a pathetic sight, but no matter, we Chiefs fans were used to suffering. We endured. We persevered. Our lone Super Bowl victory was way back in January 1970. Was that *before* electricity? No. We had electricity. I can remember watching that game on TV as a child, so we must've had electricity. Hank Stram, Len Dawson, Ed Podolak, Otis Taylor, Willie Lanier, Curly Culp, Buck Buchanan, Jan Stenerud. Wow. That *was* a long time ago, wasn't it?

Anyway, one particular Sunday I can remember sitting in the bar, at 10 AM, alone, watching yet another Chiefs game. I looked over at the end of the bar and saw another lonely, tortured soul. But this soul was wearing a Cleveland Browns jersey. Ha. The Browns had *never* won a Super Bowl. In the social hierarchy of lonely, pathetic, loser sports fans, I was one rung *above* him. One must savor the small victories.

I haven't bored you with any stories of my kids yet, so let's rectify that, shall we?

Ecstatic, the St. Louis Blues were playing the LA Kings, and the game would be televised! No more lonely sports bar scene for me. I could watch the hockey game in the comfort of my rented home. My wife volunteered at the local hospital – she got to hold babies for hours on end, which had the added benefit of scratching that itch, so no pressure on me to have a third child (yet). That evening it would just be me and the two kids, hunkered down on the floor with all manner of Legos, building blocks, and toy vehicles spread out before us. Oh yeah, and the Blues game on the telly. I hadn't seen a Blues game in quite a while, so there was eager anticipation. My kids, much too young to be hockey fans, were eager nonetheless, no doubt my emotion spilling over. *Osmosis* I think they call it.

Game starts. First period. We're building blocks and demolishing blocks. Build. Demolish. Rinse. Repeat. After a few cycles the kids get thirsty, so I'm off to the kitchen.

HE SHOOTS! HE SCORES! I sprint back to the TV. Missed it. *Heard* it. But didn't get to *see* it. No matter, I think to myself. Blues up 1-0.

Second period. My daughter, still in diapers, *needed* to be changed (it had been postponed long enough). I'm off to the bedroom to retrieve the required tools and supplies. *HE SHOOTS! HE SCORES!* Dang, missed it again. No matter, I *say* to myself. Blues now up 2-0.

Third period. My son, in the potty training phase of life, declared that he had to *go*. Wonderful, he's really catching on to this toilet thing. But... when my son tells you has to *go*, it means *go* NOW! A diaper change could be postponed. This could not. Immediate attention was required. We're off to the toilet. You know what's coming, don't you? *HE SHOOTS! HE SCORES!* (This book almost writes itself.) I could no longer muster a feeble *no matter*. "Damn!" I had missed *another* goal. So much for *watching* the Blues game.

When your son, knee-deep in potty training, has a *successful* trip to the toilet, and is rewarded with an expletive from his father... well... let's just say I had some explaining to do.

Father: "No, Danny, it wasn't you, it's the Blues game."
Son: "But Dad, aren't they *winning*?"

Well crap, even more explaining to do. Blues win 3-0.

CHAPTER 9
A KEEP EAGLE STORY

In one sentence, Keep Eagle was the USAF program to develop and test a new high Angle of Attack (AOA) departure resistance and spin recovery flight control system for the F-15E. One sentence does not do it justice, not even close. Keep Eagle consumed several years of my life, including packing up the family and moving to Lancaster, CA to monitor the high AOA flight test program at Edwards AFB. Volumes could be written about my years working this program, but I'll try to keep it short – only three humorous stories.

Prior to moving to Edwards, my primary role during Keep Eagle was to help design the new high AOA flight control laws. The design team consisted of a grand total of... *three* engineers. One guy worked on mode transitions and failure states. The other guy worked solely on linear analysis. That left me to design, simulate, and test the primary control law functions, consisting of the forward path channels (i.e. stick and pedals to control surfaces) and the feedback paths (i.e. aircraft response to control surfaces). I was busy, to be sure, but it was not a daunting task for one engineer to accomplish – no sympathy required.

[Author's note: I never understood the value of *linear* analysis at high AOA, where the aerodynamics were decidedly *non-linear*. Honestly, regardless of what the linear analysis showed or didn't show, we were still going to go fly. But I was neither making staffing decisions nor paying his salary, so, whatever.]

A large part of the design phase was having pilots evaluate the paths and gain schedules in the simulator (ugh – think GCWS all over again). The feedbacks were used to help stabilize the aircraft, and the feedback gains had to be fine-tuned to provide just enough stability, but without stifling roll performance. So, we would have the pilots hop in the sim (yes, with sim cards), we would ratchet the gains up or down, and they would tell us how the jet behaved.

During one such evaluation, the sim engineer, we'll call him Jay, inadvertently inserted a negative sign on the gain. The feedback that was supposed to help *stabilize* the jet, was now doing just the opposite, i.e. making the jet *worse* than it would've been with no feedbacks at all. Think of trying to drive your car not knowing the steering wheel was hooked up backwards – it was almost, but not quite, that bad.

To our shock and amazement, the pilot was flying with this negative gain. His only comment? It was *not as nice* and required a *bit more workload* than the previous gain set, but was still flyable. Huh? There could be only one of two explanations. Either this pilot had that elusive *golden arm*, or pilots had no need for our fancy feedbacks and gain schedules. I chose the former and continued with my design. I needed to be needed.

You may remember reading about potential EP sim sessions for flight testing. Keep Eagle was one of those programs where they were used extensively. A high AOA flight test program was well-suited for EP sim sessions because the airspeeds were generally low and the altitudes high, so there was a relative abundance of time to think about things, make calls, and apply recovery procedures. We also used these sim sessions to help train new engineers, so the first time they saw something unexpected, or the first time they had to make a call, was not during an actual flight. What a concept, huh? A luxury not afforded to me, but at least I could help rectify that for younger engineers.

One of the *failures* we used to intentionally confuse the engineers was to have the pilot apply controls differently than how directed to do so. Standing next to the cockpit in the simulator dome, when the test conductor relayed a command to the pilot, I would lean over and whisper to the pilot either not to do it, or do it in the *wrong* direction. It was a *blind* test for the control room, and was actually great training for new engineers, as it was all too easy to see things happen as expected time and time again, and become complacent. If the test conductor called for stick *left*, and the engineers saw the stick move *right*, or *not move at all*, it made them *think*. What was wrong? Did the pilot not hear the call? Was the instrumentation correct? Were the strip charts setup properly? Was something actually wrong with the jet? All of these scenarios had to be considered. The engineers *had* to come up with a response and relay it to the pilot, or else risk losing the jet (a *simulated* loss of course).

Well, as luck would have it, Flood was the pilot for that particular EP session. Yes, Flood. The very pilot who had so many issues with left versus right stick, left versus right pedal, etc. The man with a 50% success rate, simply because there were only *two* options to choose from. I stood next to the cockpit, grinning. This was gonna be *fun*, at least for me – I was no longer the newb.

It came time to do the secret *pilot puts in opposite stick* thing. I had already pre-briefed Flood to do the opposite when that time came. He *knew* what I wanted, but when the test conductor made the call, he became a tortured soul. The test conductor said, "Stick right." I shook my head and whispered, "No." Flood was a wreck. You could almost hear the neurons colliding inside his brain. No doubt in a fit of total confusion and frustration, he just flung the stick in any direction, hoping and praying for one of his 50% success rate miracles. I was biting my lip, trying not to laugh. Success! Flood got the *proper* direction – meaning in this case *left*, or the *wrong* direction. That blind squirrel had found his nut.

But now was the even funnier part. The engineers in the control room all knew Flood was the pilot. They were all well aware of his 50% at best success rate. So when the test conductor called for stick right and they saw the stick move left, *they* became the confused and tortured souls. Was something wrong with the instrumentation, strip charts, or the aircraft? Or was this one of those blind EPs? Or was this simply Flood being Flood?

Enough of the sim sessions, now on to real flight testing...

Several of us engineers were monitoring a test flight one day, busying ourselves with watching strip charts and digital displays, monitoring our key parameters, and making calls to the test conductor who would then relay the information to the pilot.

[Author's note: We lowly technology engineers were not allowed to make radio calls directly to the pilot. Never. Ever. The reason given was supposedly because procedures dictated there only be a single voice transmitting to the pilot to avoid potential confusion. Understood. Sure. Whatever. The real reason, we all knew, was pilots didn't want to hear what we engineers really thought.]

On this particular flight we did some intentional departures at a relatively fast airspeed. And when I say *we were doing*, yes, yes, I know that it was the *pilots* actually in the aircraft performing the maneuver, not the engineers. But it was *our* test point. We engineers wrote the TIS. So, I'm going to continue saying *we* did the maneuver. Deal with it as you wish. And when I say *departure*, it's not like a train leaving the station. A *departure* means the aircraft is no longer in control, or how we engineers explain it to pilots, *the pointy end is not going forward anymore.*

Intentional departures were where we asked the pilot to completely ignore the Flight Manual and do some foolish control inputs. Wait a minute, there should be a reflective pause here... *Ask the pilot to ignore the Flight Manual? Ask the pilot to apply foolish control inputs?* Is this pilot heaven? Nirvana?

Speaking of pilots ignoring the Flight Manual, here are two appropriate jokes...

One of the most important skills that a pilot must develop is the skill to ignore those things that were designed by non-pilots to get the pilot's attention.

The aircraft g-limits are only there in case there is another flight by that particular airplane. If subsequent flights do not appear likely, there are no g-limits.

Back to the story...

The pilot performed this prescribed *intentional* departure maneuver, and sure enough the jet did depart from controlled flight, pretty much as expected. Stupid in equals stupid out, I suppose. But what was *not* expected was one of the engines stalled and stagnated (meaning it would not recover on its own after the departure was over and the jet had settled back to normal flying attitude, pointy end going forward). Quick *pop* stalls that self-recovered were common during high AOA testing, but not this deeper stall that resulted in an engine stagnation.

To put this in some perspective, we performed over a hundred intentional departures and spins during the course of Keep Eagle flight testing, and had only *one* engine anomaly. One. In eighteen months of high AOA flight testing, this one stall/stagnation event was it. The F-15 engines and inlets performed incredibly well. Given the history of high AOA flight testing of fighter aircraft, this is not some meaningless statistic.

[Author's note: I would almost consider giving some credit to propulsion/inlet engineers, but it would likely just go to their heads and then they might consider writing a book or some other such nonsense...]

You may recall I led off this chapter by saying this was a *humorous* story. Is having an engine stall and stagnate *funny?* No. Is asking a pilot to intentionally do something foolish *funny?* No. Not at all. Well, maybe the latter is funny, but just a little bit...

Here's the humorous part. We first learned about the engine event because we heard (over the headsets) the *pilot* call out the engine had stalled. We were all expecting, given the situation, that our resident propulsion engineer, we'll call him Kevin, would've made some sort of call to the test conductor. Nothing. Crickets. Crickets I say.

[Author's note: You should understand something here. The reason we spend years of effort and millions of dollars to instrument a test aircraft is so we engineers, who monitor the test flights in real time, can see what's happening to the jet <u>before</u> the aircrew see it or feel it.]

Upon hearing about the engine stall from the pilot, I instinctively turned around to see what our resident propulsion engineer friend could possibly be up to, and I found that his headset had slipped down, so the large padded band that normally sits on top of his head was now covering his eyes. He had a strip chart machine in front of him with eight pens showing various engine data parameters, some of which no doubt were moving all helter skelter due to the stall, but he could see *nothing. Two's blind* in pilot speak.

Our resident propulsion engineer friend had but *one* job to do. *One* strip chart machine to watch. *One* call to make – "Throttles Idle" (yes, even I knew what his call was supposed to be). He practiced this during multiple sim sessions. He rehearsed this during *every* pre-flight briefing. Yet the one time we needed him to actually do his job, he was blinded by a headset strap. In today's vernacular we might call this a *wardrobe failure* (back in the 1990s we had no clue what that phrase meant).

No shortage of grief was heaped upon our resident propulsion engineer friend, but Kevin was a good guy and took it all in stride. It was funny. Well, funny that it happened to him and not to me.

This story shows it's not always engineer versus pilot banter, sometimes it can be engineer versus engineer. Although as a general rule we engineers try to stick together and limit such inter-discipline ridicule to only that which is absolutely required.

Let's end with an engineer joke...

Hello. I'm an aerospace engineer. To save time let's assume that I'm never wrong.

Photo of F-15E#1 (tail number 86-0183) during the Keep Eagle program, circa 1994. Photo credit USAF.

F-15E Project Keep Eagle patch.

CHAPTER 10
CHINA LAKE – A TRAVEL STORY

I did my fair share of traveling for work. Some good trips. Some not so good trips. Some bad trips. Sounds like LSD maybe? Anyway, here's the story from my *worst trip ever*. I travelled to NAS China Lake to monitor AV-8B AMRAAM flight testing for the Marines. This was actually not my trip. This was supposed to be another engineer's trip, but at the last minute the guy's wife got sick so he couldn't go.

Allow me to vent for a moment. One of the worst qualities management at my company had was the belief that all engineers were essentially the same. In math you would write this equation as:

Engineer A = Engineer B = Engineer C

We were just heads on an organization chart. So, when Engineer A couldn't make his assigned travel due to personal issues, they'd just assign Engineer B (in this case me) to fill in for him. No problem, right? Sure, if they ignore the fact that Engineer A was the *only* engineer to work on the AV-8B AMRAAM project leading up to this point. And never mind that Engineer B (me) had *never* worked on *any* AV-8B project, thus having *zero* experience with that jet. But that's OK, because Engineer B (me) had done flight test monitoring before. Who cares that all of that flight test monitoring experience was on the F-15. In effect, not only did Engineer A = Engineer B according to management, but apparently Jet A = Jet B. Sheesh.

In the medical world, it would read something like this. A patient is scheduled for brain surgery. The brain surgeon calls in sick that morning. Is the surgery rescheduled? No. The hospital checks the staff's schedules and finds a resident proctologist who happens to be free all morning. What luck! They assign the proctologist to do the brain surgery, because after all, both are medically trained professionals. Doctor A = Doctor B.

OK, sorry, I'm back now...

For some reason this story seems to be best read in a bulletized list format (probably the engineer in me). And for some other strange reason, I find some comfort writing this in third person. Subliminally hoping this happened to somebody else, not me, perhaps?

- Ron arrived at work and found out at 8 AM he's supposed to be on a plane at noon to cover flight testing on an aircraft that he's not familiar with (Jet A = Jet B) at a base he's never been to.
- Secretary switched reservations to my name. It was not a non-stop flight – no big deal he thought at the time.
- Ron quickly collected some papers, went home, and packed a bag.
- Ron rushed frantically to get to the airport on time. Miraculously he arrived at the gate just in time to board (luckily this was pre 9/11 days, so getting through the airport security was not a huge issue).
- At the gate, Ron learned the flight would be several hours delayed (pre cell phone days, so there was no way to know of the delay in advance).
- Ron had newly discovered *spare* time, was able to read the TWD and reviewed the test plan. After just a few hours sitting in an airport, Ron apparently became an AV-8B AMRAAM flying qualities *expert* (Engineer A = Engineer B).
- The flight finally got airborne. Southwest Airlines. Ron had never flown Southwest Airlines before. Ron was hungry. Ron was expecting a meal on the plane (back when some airlines actually served meals).
- In lieu of a meal, Ron got a half-ounce bag of peanuts and a half can of Coke. It's OK, Ron convinced himself. He'll grab something to eat at the airport during one of the stops.
- The plane landed in Tulsa for Stop 1. Hungry Ron prepared to disembark. The flight attendant announced that due to the delay getting started, this would be a quick-turn – saying they would only be stopped long enough to board additional passengers. *Nobody* was allowed off the plane.
- The plane took off again. Another half-ounce bag of peanuts and another half a Coke.
- The plane landed in Phoenix for Stop 2. Guess what? Yep, another quick-turn. By this point Ron was getting *real* hungry.
- The plane took off yet again. Another half-ounce bag of peanuts and another half a Coke. It was now close to 10 PM his time and all Ron's had to eat or drink since 6:30 in the morning is one and a half ounces of peanuts and one and a half cans of Coke. The combined action of salt, caffeine, and turbulence wreaked havoc on his stomach.
- After all the stops and delays, Ron finally arrived in Ontario, CA at 10 PM (midnight his time).
- Ontario, CA is small airport. Rental car counters normally close at 9 PM. Ron did not know that. How would he? He's never been there. Ron thought Ontario was a province in *Canada*.

- Ron found one agent packing up, but still present – but it's the *wrong* rental company per McDonnell Douglas travel rules. Somehow he was able to get a car anyway. Ron contemplated the hassle of explaining to travel accounting why he did not use the company preferred rental car company.
- Ron left Ontario around 11 PM, started the drive to Ridgecrest.
- Ron looked at a map (pre GPS days) and decided it would be faster to continue north on two-lane roads (certainly no traffic at this time of night), as opposed to going west to Palmdale, and then going north on Hwy 14. It was an entirely logical decision.
- Ron continued approximately 30 miles north and suddenly came up on a myriad of yellow signs and flashing lights. The road was closed ahead.
- Ron turned around, drove south approximately 30 miles, then west to Palmdale, then up Hwy 14 north. Logic sucks.
- Ron arrived in Ridgecrest at 2 AM (yes, 4 AM his time). Did he mention the pre-flight briefing was scheduled for 6 AM with an 8 AM takeoff?
- Ron checked into the hotel. The only room left was a smoking room.
- Ron climbed into bed and slept fitfully for a few hours. The pillow absolutely reeked of cigarette smoke. He awoke with a massive headache.
- Ron hopped in the shower, only to find hundreds of red bumps on his legs and torso. Yep, bed bugs. He's heard of them, but never actually seen them. Wasn't quite sure if they really existed. Now know they do, in fact, exist.
- Ron got to NAS China Lake at 5:30 AM. No breakfast – the hotel was much too cheap to have a buffet. No fast food restaurants were open yet. Why would they be? It's not even 6 AM yet.
- Ron's name was not on the approved visitor list at the guard shack. Of course not, why would it be? The other guy's name was on the list (that would be Engineer A). The guard had no idea who I was. Of course not, why would he know me? We called the local McDonnell point of contact – too early, he's not at work yet. Of course not, why would he be there? He doesn't attend pre-flight briefings, especially those scheduled for 6 AM.
- Ron finally got past the guard (don't remember details). He had never been to China Lake, had no clue where he's going. It was pitch black outside. Of course it was pitch black, it's not even 6 AM yet. That's already been established.
- Ron finally found the McDonnell building, entered and wandered around. Guess what? Nobody there. Of course you fool, it's 6 AM.
- Ron finally figured out the briefing was in the *Navy* building, which was located across the ramp (a building he has *never* been in and a ramp he has *never* walked on – just so you know).
- Ron arrived 10 minutes late for the briefing. Pilots and engineers, most of whom he'd never even seen before, gave him a *who the hell are you and why are you late* look of disgust. Ron sat down, scratched his legs, and kept his damn mouth shut. (If you had ever arrived late at one of Dragon's briefings, you would know what Ron's talking about.)

- The briefing went remarkably well. They asked Ron one question. He replied, "I don't know," followed by more looks of disgust. They thought, at present, Ron was a worthless lump of human matter with no possible means of contributing anything positive to this mission. They were not wrong. Engineer A = Engineer B was not looking so good right now, regardless of what company management might have thought.
- The briefing ended. Ron went back to the McDonnell building and found an empty desk. What a dump. The McDonnell building at NAS China Lake made the trailers at Edwards AFB look like the Taj Mahal.
- 30 minutes until engine start-up. Ron was hungry. Should be enough time. He drove off base and got fast food for breakfast – mmm, good.
- Ron got back to the base at the same time all the people working normal hours arrived. He now had to wait in a long line at the gate.
- Ron finally got through the gate and back to the Navy building. The door to the telemetry (TM) room had a Unicam lock. Guess what? Nobody told him the code. Of course not, nobody knows him from Adam.
- Ron banged on the door. No answer. He banged some more. The TM room technician finally heard and let him in, but not before giving him that *who are you and why are you bothering me* look. Of course he gave him that look – he's never seen him before. Obviously, he had no idea that Ron was that illustrious McDonnell Douglas *Engineer B* he had no doubt heard so much about.
- Ron entered the TM room and discovered that the jet's engine was already running and TM was up. He was late again. More looks of disgust. At least his belly was full.
- Ron found his strip charts, sat down, scratched his legs, and started to figure out the headphone, microphone, and strip chart set up. No, it was not the same setup used at Edwards AFB. Of course not, why would it be? This a *Navy* base and a *Marine* test program.
- A minute or two later a Navy engineer realized some engine instrumentation parameter wasn't working, and it just happened to be on the mission critical list. Flight was cancelled for the day.
- Ron sat there, completely stunned. He couldn't decide whether to be happy or sad. All he could think about was how blissfully unaware he was sitting at his desk in St. Louis the previous morning – having absolutely no clue what wrath the following 24 hours would bring.
- Ron wandered back to the McDonnell building. What a dump.

I've been told that every story should have a redeeming quality. A silver lining perhaps? Something? Sorry, not this one. And that shouldn't be too surprising, given it's earned the label *my worst trip ever*, which is saying something. I guess the one non-terrible thing I could say about this China Lake trip was it made all of my other trips look good by comparison.

In 30+ years working on the F-15, I have had some good trips. Some of the more notable destinations included Nellis AFB (Las Vegas, NV), Eglin AFB (Ft. Walton Beach, FL), Arnold AFB (Tullahoma, TN), Hickam AFB (Honolulu, HI), Wright Patterson AFB (Dayton, OH), Langley AFB (Langley, VA), NASA Ames (Moffett Field, CA), Kadena AFB (Okinawa, Japan), and Taejon, South Korea.

The problem with good trips, productive trips, is that you don't get as many humorous stories. So sorry, nothing more to report. Best I can do is a photo...

Photo of the author (center) with F-15 pilot Herc (left) and F-15 SPO engineer Hugh Darsey (right) at Kadena AFB, Okinawa, circa 2002. Luckily for me, troubleshooting a jet requires neither vertical stature nor perfect eyesight. Photo credit unknown.

CHAPTER 11
LIFE IN THE DESERT – PART DEUX

"Engineers have more words for screwing up than the Inuit have words for snow."
　　– Pierce Nichol

Much later in my career the desert beckoned me yet again – this time for a long-term (about 20 month) stint while testing the Saudi F-15SA with a new fly-by-wire flight control system. Same jet on the outside, but new flight control brains on the inside. This testing was conducted out of the Boeing hangars at Palmdale, but utilized the same Edwards AFB test ranges the original F-15A model used 40 years earlier and the F-15E model used 25 years earlier. The more things change, the more they stay the same?

One thing that was different compared to F-15E testing 25 years earlier was there were a lot more engineers (and one pilot) of female persuasion. Two will be mentioned a bit later. Another was one of our test conductors, her call sign was *Def*. Engineers with call signs – aww, how cute is that? Anyway, during this twenty month assignment I learned just how well the female engineers (and one pilot) could dish out barbs to their male counterparts. This brought an entirely new dimension to the banter between engineers and pilots. Game on indeed.

Anyway, a couple of stories from my Palmdale tour of duty are worth sharing...

It's just sand...

During my long-term *commitment* to Palmdale, other engineers in my aero group came out for short-term three month stints to gain flight test experience and assist in flight monitoring duties. One such engineer, we'll call her Beth, was coming out to Palmdale for the first time. I was home in St. Louis for the weekend, so we arranged to take the same flight from St. Louis to LA (Burbank) – that way she could give me a ride to my Lancaster *home* in her rental car, and I could show her the way around the Antelope Valley. It was a win-win scenario. Mutually beneficial and all that.

We landed at Burbank, de-planed, and stood, waiting for bags at baggage claim. Beth has this huge grin on her face. I don't know about you, but most people I know don't experience immense pleasure waiting at baggage claim. This matter would require further inquiry. The exchange went something like this:

Ron: What's up? Why are you smiling?
Beth: We're in *Hollywood.*
Ron: Yes, Beth. We're in Hollywood.
Beth: Ooh, this is *so* exciting.

We got the bags and the rental car. Beth started driving north on I-5 towards the Antelope Valley. A bit later we were on I-14 north of LA, but still not over the pass yet, an area where the scenery transitions from dirt and concrete to dirt and sand. Beth was still grinning from ear to ear. Another exchange ensued:

Ron: *Now* what are you smiling about?
Beth: Ooh, this is so *pretty*.
Ron: What? Pretty? Beth – it's sand and dirt. Dirt and sand. As far as you can see. It's all brown, just different shades of brown. How on earth can this be *pretty*?
Beth: Ooh, I know, I know, but it's so pretty.

We crossed over the pass and started down into the Antelope Valley. From this vantage point we can see Palmdale in front of us, Lancaster in the distance, and the dry lake beds further off in the distance. Being the ever dutiful tour guide, I pointed out all of this to Beth. We had another quite similar exchange:

Beth: Ooh, this is so pretty.
Ron: Beth, we've had this discussion already. It's just sand, as far as you can see. And if you drive another hundred miles it's just more sand, as far as you can see. It is not pretty. It's brown. Everything in this valley is just brown.
Beth: I don't care, I still think it's pretty.

Defeated. Exhausted. *OK Beth, it's pretty.* Later that evening I called my wife and told her about our trip over the pass. She berated me for being such a downer to Beth, especially given that it was her first time in SoCal. I felt terrible. Not really, but it sounds good to say I felt terrible.

The dirt bike...

Several of the flight test engineers (FTEs) assigned to Palmdale were twenty-something single males. Four or five of them got together and rented a very large, and very nice house, which then logically became known as *the FTE house.* The house sat on a three acre, barbed wire fenced lot, consisting of – yes, you guessed it... sand.

I was at the FTE house one evening, just hanging out with the *young-uns* (what my southern Granny used to call her five grandchildren). There was a discussion underway about how nice it would be if we had my 4-wheeler ATV there to ride around in the sand, instead of it sitting at home in St. Louis doing nothing – useless as a wet fart in a paper bag. Or maybe if we had a go-kart? Something, *anything*, to take advantage of the space afforded by a three acre sandlot with precious little adult supervision.

A week or so of scouring the local Craigslist ads was all it took to scratch that itch – a small, used Honda dirt bike at a very reasonable price. Seems the guy's kids had outgrown it. Funny, because it fit me *perfectly*. I made the purchase, strapped it in the bed of my truck, and called one of the young-uns at the FTE house to see if they would be home, because I had a *package* to deliver. As I pull into the back yard next to the garage (it's all sand so you could drive anywhere), one of the FTEs, we'll call him Chad, comes out and makes the astute observation, "Um Ron. That looks like a *dirt bike* in the bed of your truck." Yes, Chad. Yes it is.

It took no more than two minutes to unload the bike, fire it up, and start doing laps in the sand. What a blast. For some unknown reason, there was a very large pile of packed sand in the middle of the back yard, probably 4 or 5 feet tall. Perfect. Terrain. Nearby there were some cinder blocks and a scrap piece of plywood. Presto! A ramp begging to be jumped. Within minutes, that once featureless desert sandlot now had *features*. It wasn't a full-up motocross course by any means, but it would certainly offer some variety and entertainment.

Dirt bikes could be fun. Dirt bikes on loose sand could be, umm... challenging. Traction was not something in abundant supply when riding on loose sand. When you gave the bike more gas, the back end could get rather squirrelly. Keeping the bike upright while trying to slow down could also be a bit of a challenge. And don't forget about the barbed wire fence. If you couldn't get the bike slowed down or turned on the loose sand, well then that fence was going to end up being your companion, an uninvited guest.

I came to find out the F-15SA flight test manager at Palmdale, we'll call her Leigh, was not entirely thrilled to learn that we now had a dirt bike taking up residence in the FTE garage. We recently had two maintenance guys get hurt while riding motorcycles on the roads around Palmdale. Leigh was already struggling trying to maintain an adequate maintenance staff to support the three flight test jets, and having guys out on medical leave due to motorcycle accidents was not helping. And then Ron shows up at the FTE house with a dirt bike.

I think Leigh thought more of me, as in an assumed level of maturity, given I was old enough to be the fathers of each of the FTEs living at the FTE house. I guess I disappointed her. She threatened to kill me. I hoped it was an idle threat, but was not certain. Sorry about all that, Leigh. But we sure did have fun with that dirt bike. And to my knowledge, nobody got hurt while riding it, even though it did get put down on the sand several times. Loose sand was a fickle bitch – it made it hard to ride, but if you did dump the bike it would offer relative softness to break the fall, for both you and the bike.

And now, several years later, that little Honda dirt bike resides at my brother's farm, located in the rolling hills of northwest Missouri. A place, by the way, with no sand, lots of green grass, and copious traction. Did I mention no sand? Green?

Molten beans...

Another nice thing about the FTE house was it was a great place to have parties. The twenty-something single male FTEs did not disappoint. There was also a fire pit built into the ground in the back yard. During one particular party they had a nice bonfire going – and with nothing but sand in the entire yard there were no issues relative to fire containment.

Several of us engineers were standing by the fire, enjoying the evening and shooting the breeze. In passing, I asked them if they had ever seen a can of beans blown up in a fire. Their collective response was essentially, "No way. Does that really work?" Oh yeah, it works. So, we head to the pantry to find something worthy of blowing up. Chili beans work the best, but they had none. A generic can of bean soup would have to suffice.

A trough in the coals was hollowed out and the can nestled deep inside, laying on its side. Within a minute, sizzling could be heard emanating from inside the can. After another minute or so, BOOM! Not a huge BOOM, mind you, but enough to convince the young-uns the concept was indeed valid. Hot molten bean soup spewed from each end of the can.

[Author's note: The cool part of this experiment is the technology. The can does not split or burst along its side, as you might think. The structural weak links in a tin can are the crimped lids on either end. So, as pressure builds up, the crimps eventually *unfold* and the ends go flying out, followed close behind by a hot mass of beans. And since only the ends blow, you can control the direction of the spewed contents by the orientation of the can in the fire. It's all very scientific, even if not *aerodynamic*. And remember, engineers are really just kids who never outgrew their Lincoln logs, Tinker Toys, and Legos – designing stuff, building stuff, and then destroying stuff. And also remember, it is the obligation of older engineers to pass their knowledge and wisdom to younger engineers. Circle of life and all that. This was my duty and I was not going to take it lightly.]

One of the engineers watching all of this, we'll call him Jeff, was absolutely mesmerized. A single BOOM was nowhere near enough to satisfy him. He dragged me back into the pantry to look for more cans. Alas, there were no can goods with appropriate contents – remember there were five twenty-something male FTEs living at this house, so bare shelves was not much of a surprise. It's too bad cans of beer didn't go BOOM?

Given the successful concept validation phase, Jeff insists we make a run to the grocery store to get more *ammo*. Well, to come clean, and as you might have surmised anyway, there was some alcohol involved in the preceding BOOM scenario. Neither Jeff nor I should be driving, and we both knew it – yes, we were kids that never outgrew the Lego phase of our lives, but we were not *stupid* kids. And at just that moment, as if on cue, who arrives at the party? Beth. Yes, the "ooh, this is so exciting" Beth. I know of no other.

Jeff pleaded our case, trying to convince Beth we needed her to drive us to the grocery store for two reasons; 1) because she can *still* drive, and 2) because she is on a short-term trip and can charge meal costs on her expense report. A very logical argument. Entirely fact based. Somewhat to our shock, she agreed.

Scanning the canned goods aisle, Jeff pestered me with questions like, "are *pinto* beans better than *garbanzo* beans?", "are chili beans in *hot* sauce better than chili beans in *mild* sauce?", and "are cheaper store brand beans OK?" I tried to convince Jeff that, while blowing up cans of beans was indeed a highly *technical* endeavor, it was not an *exact* science, and thus answers to his pressing questions probably didn't exist, at least in the current literature of the day. Puzzled, but satisfied, Jeff grabbed an assortment of beans, and we made our way to the cash register. Beth did her duty and made the purchase. Hopefully Beth's manager wouldn't look too closely at her receipts and discover her *meal* on Saturday night consisted of a dozen or so cans of beans. Oh yeah, and a 12-pack of beer too.

Beth did her *other* duty, chauffeur, and we arrived back at the FTE house. Beth and I stayed inside to talk with some folks, but Jeff was nowhere to be seen. After a few minutes I ventured outside. Jeff approached from the darkness with a huge grin on his face and nonchalantly announced he had just put five cans of beans in the fire. FIVE cans! At the same time? Are you kidding me? Dumbfounded, but still grinning, he gave me that *did I do something wrong* look. We stand... and watch... and wait... We could do nothing else. It was too late for a *knock-it-off* call. This maneuver had started. There was no stopping it. There was no going back. We had stepped off the proverbial diving platform and the only thing left to do was hit the water. We stepped back to a more, ahem, *manageable* distance. After all, we weren't stupid, as we've already established.

BOOM... BOOM... BOOM... BOOM... and BOOM! (All in fairly rapid succession.)

We approached the fire pit. There were molten beans and hot embers strewn out from both sides of the pit, along with the odd tin can remnant and neatly unfolded lids that could still be found.

By all measures, it was a very successful night of legume demolition. Embers actually shot out 50 feet from the fire pit. 50 feet! Wait, 50 feet? How did we know? Because we *measured* it (it's what engineers do). Much grinning ensued. Note this smashed the previous record of 35 feet, set by my son and his friends during a trip to my brother's farm.

You might think the molten beans story would end at this point. *Au contraire mon ami.* That's French for *keep reading...*

Jeff and I collected the strewn embers and returned them back to the fire pit. After policing up the area as best we could, we retired to the patio to sip a beer and revel in our feats of pyrotechnic strength. The only things missing were the two of us talking loudly, interrupting each other, and arms flailing in the air. We were, after all, engineers, not pilots. We possessed the ability to discuss our incredible personal exploits in a calm, civil manner.

In the midst of our revelry, some unknown couple strode to the edge of the fire pit. A romantic sight, the hand-holding couple silhouetted against the glow from the embers. After a few minutes they strolled back to the house.

And then it happened. BOOM!

I turned to Jeff, wide eyed in utter disbelief, "*Jeff, you said you put FIVE cans in the fire!*" Jeff turned to me, also wide eyed, and shrieked, "*I did! I did! Or did I put SIX cans in the fire? I can't remember!*"

This whole *six* versus *five* cans could not be a coincidence, could it? All things happen for a reason, right? It had to be a reference to Clint Eastwood in the movie *Dirty Harry*. The confusion over six versus five cans had to have been Jeff's subliminal way of reliving that *Dirty Harry* moment:

"Did he put *six* cans of beans in the fire or only *five*? Well to tell you the truth, in all this excitement, I kind of lost track myself. But being that these are store brand hot chili beans, the most powerful beans in the world, and would blow your head clean off, you've got to ask yourself one question: 'Do I feel lucky?' Well, do ya, punk?"

The entire episode did not add to Leigh's assumed level of maturity in me. It took months and months of hard work and dedication to redeem my standing in her eyes. It was worth it.

R2LB: If you can smile when things go wrong, you likely have someone in mind to blame.

F-15SA Flight Test patches.

CHAPTER 12
HAPPY HOUR

I need to preface this chapter with another joke and a rule to live by...

Q. What is the difference between a fighter pilot and a pig?
A. The pig doesn't turn into a fighter pilot when it's drunk.

R2LB: Sometimes too much to drink is not enough.

I won't say pilots and engineers on remote flight test assignments drink. I also won't say they don't. I will say happy hour is something that is eagerly awaited by some, especially on Fridays after a long week. What time each discipline shows up at happy hour is evidence to the amount of work required of each discipline.

Here's how a typical Friday would go:

- 0700 Pre-flight briefing.
- 0800 Aircrew step to the jet.
- 0900 Ground ops complete, aircraft takes off. Mission begins.
- 1230 Test points completed, aircraft lands. Mad scramble to scarf lunch.
- 1300 Post-flight briefing.
- 1400 Briefing complete. Everybody returns to their desks and tries to get the work done they couldn't do before because they were tied up watching somebody *else* fly *their* jet.

About 15 minutes later a WSO would stop by my desk and say, "Hey, we're pushing to XYZ [insert name of local bar] at 1430 for happy hour." "What? I haven't even *started* my flight report yet." WSO replies, "Huh. Sucks being you. See ya."

About an hour or so later a pilot would stop by my desk and say, "Hey, we're pushing to XYZ at 1530 for happy hour." "What? I haven't *finished* my flight report yet." Pilot replies, "Huh. Sucks being you. See ya."

[Author's note. At first I felt somewhat honored the aircrew would ask me to join them for happy hour. Then later I found out why. Apparently, me, sitting at the bar with them, made them look better by comparison. No proof of that of course, but that was the theory. Since pilots and WSOs had a perverse habit of buying me beers quite often, I was not going to argue that theory. You have to know who butters your bread. In other words, when I walked into a bar for happy hour, late, and there was a beer waiting for me, I was not going to say something like, "I'd prefer a nice autumnal mead instead." (VCR)]

There were two reports that had to be written after each test mission. The lead engineer on the mission wrote, unsurprisingly, the *engineering* flight report. The pilot wrote, you guessed it, the *pilot* flight report. The engineering flight report was a detailed accounting of what was flown during the mission and the results, and involved transcribing hand-written notes taken during the mission into a coherent and comprehensive document. It was not a trivial task. It could take several hours to write a report such as this. This report would be read by potentially a hundred or more people. (Potentially 95 or more people than will read this book.)

The pilot flight report, on the other hand, was only as coherent and comprehensive as time before the afternoon push to happy hour allowed. In fact, if one ever saw what appeared to be a mere shell of a flight report, with scant few details, one could be assured it was from a Friday test mission.

Many test pilots, after seeing their brethren WSOs head to the bar for happy hour mere minutes after landing, complained bitterly about the *onerous* task of writing their report. If writing a report was not bad enough, think of having to write a report while knowing your WSO, the very guy who was sitting in your pit during the mission, was already at the bar tipping a few back. Test pilot – it was decidedly *not* a profession for the weak-willed.

ER: When a pilot complains about *their* problem, it will likely become *your* problem.

Having grown tired of the incessant complaining, I took it upon myself to help them out. Remember, engineers *solve* problems. Rather than asking the pilot to describe each maneuver and each set of results, I devised a scheme that offered them a list of canned maneuver descriptions, complete with a corresponding results section. All a pilot would have to do is copy/paste the suitable text and then check the appropriate box. Below is a sample of what I came up with for them.

Maneuver:
- o Pilot performed the maneuver as directed per the card.
- o Pilot performed maneuver to the right when it was prescribed as a left maneuver, but otherwise performed the maneuver flawlessly.
- o Pilot performed maneuver with full control input when it was prescribed as a half control input, but otherwise performed the maneuver flawlessly.
- o Pilot performed maneuver with pedal when the maneuver was to be performed with stick, but otherwise performed the maneuver flawlessly.
- o Pilot attempted to perform the maneuver per the card, but the card was so poorly written that execution was nearly impossible.
- o Pilot read the card, found himself perplexed, and did something else.
- o Pilot read the card, understood it, but opted to do something else anyway.
- o Pilot did not read the card, but performed a miraculous feat of airmanship nonetheless.
- o Gross buffoonery ensued whilst airborne.

Maneuver Results:

- o Typical.
- o Atypical.
- o You gotta see this.
- o You ain't gonna believe this.
- o I'm not doing *that* again. *Ever.*

Now just a couple dozen clicks in the check mark boxes, and *presto* the pilot flight report is done. Heck, you might even be able to make it to the bar *before* the WSOs do. Not likely, but possible.

Dragon   Ron

Speaking of miraculous feats of airmanship, below are two standouts from a few of my test pilot buddies...

A Spoons takeoff...

Spoons performed a takeoff with the speedbrake *extended.* The speedbrake is a device used to slow the aircraft down, typically used during landings (see earlier photo of F-15E#2). A takeoff, in marked contrast, is an event where the pilot (with a massive amount of help from the engines) is trying to *accelerate* to flying speed, not slow down. Think of performing a takeoff with the speedbrake extended as similar to a boat trying to leave the harbor without first pulling up the anchor.

You may wonder how we engineers knew Spoons had the speedbrake extended. Behold the wonders of aircraft tracking cameras and video monitors. We sat in the control room, in our comfy but boring 1g chairs, and watched the entire episode on the jumbotron monitor. Facts don't lie. Video doesn't lie. Way to go Spoons.

Thankfully the engines are powerful enough to overcome the added drag of the speedbrake, so the takeoff was a success. Spoons later claimed he was merely performing that elusive *speedbrake extended* takeoff test point that was buried somewhere deep in the TIS. In the new pilot report format mentioned above, I would've checked the box "gross buffoonery". Spoons, however, would've claimed the box "performed a miraculous feat of airmanship nonetheless" as a more accurate assessment.

A Dragon landing...

This is a topic that simply must be preceded by jokes:

> *There are three simple rules for making a smooth landing: unfortunately, no one knows what they are.*

> *A good landing is one you can walk away from.*
> *A great landing is one where you can use the airplane again.*

Dragon has always had a reputation of not being able to land the F-15 smoothly. In fact when he touches down, the word of choice is typically *PRANG*. We engineers got skilled enough to tell who was flying just by watching the load factor trace on the strip charts at landing. Right at the point of main wheel touchdown, the load factor typically jumps a bit, measuring the instantaneous deceleration at impact, and then smoothes out as the aircraft slows down and the weight settles on the landing gear. For a typical Dragon landing, the load factor jumps a LOT at the point of main wheel touchdown – in fact *touchdown* is pretty misleading, as it would be more like *slam* down. Do a YouTube search on *aircraft carrier landings* and you will get an appreciation.

During one particular flight, Dragon, seeing he had plenty of fuel remaining, decided to do a few touch and goes. A touch and go was when the pilot flew the jet all the way down to main wheel touchdown, but then added power to get airborne again, as opposed to lowering the nose and slowing to a stop during a normal landing.

Sure, Dragon, don't mind us engineers, who obviously have nothing else to do but watch you do touch and goes. No, really, we're more than happy to have you waste our time. It's not like we're eager to debrief the mission and get back to real work or anything.

Basically this is Dragon's way of saying, "Hey look at me, I'm flying the jet and you're not." Plus he has an audience. A *captive* audience. We *have* to watch. (At least we're getting paid to watch.)

The first touch and go was a typical Dragon *prang*. Big spike in load factor. Easy to see. Junkman was in the back seat. He said nothing on hot mike. If I were in the back seat it would've no doubt rattled my teeth – I would've said *something*. But nothing. Not even a grunt or moan. But you must understand, Junkman had been flying with Dragon for *years*. This was nothing new to him. "Nice landing sir" was the expression of the day.

The second touch and go was not typical Dragon. Smooth as glass. We could not even discern on the load factor strip chart the point at which main wheel touchdown actually occurred. Yeah, it was *that* smooth. Amazing. Had Dragon improved? Had he turned the corner? Was his reputation as *King of Prang* now a thing of the past?

The third and final landing was a touchdown followed by a full stop rollout. *PRANG!* Ahh, now there's the Dragon we all knew and loved. That second smooth-as-glass touch and go must've been an aberration.

The mission debrief concluded without any mention of the landings from Dragon, or from us. Some things are just left unspoken. Note Junkman had to miss debrief due to other commitments, the significance of which wasn't realized at the time.

A few days later I happened to be over in the Flight Ops area talking with Junkman. In passing I mentioned the anomaly of Dragon's *magical* second touch and go landing. Junkman chuckled and told me the *real* story, which was Dragon let *him* fly the second touch and go from the back seat. Well, that certainly would've been an interesting piece of information to know at the time.

R2LB: The facts, although interesting, are irrelevant.

Peedawg giggles...

A portion of the F-15SA high AOA flight test program involved testing at large *negative* AOAs. This was accomplished by rolling inverted (upside down), pushing forward on the stick to achieve negative AOA, and then performing a maneuver, typically a roll with pedal or lateral stick. While at negative AOA, the aircrew are experiencing negative g's, i.e. instead of having gravity and/or positive g's pull them down into their seats, they are being lifted/pushed up out of their seats. The only thing keeping them in their seats during negative g's are the harness and shoulder straps.

During one such mission with Flood in the front seat and Peedawg in the back, Flood discovered that his water bottle, located in the lower leg pocket of his flight suit, was not sealed well. As he pushed to negative AOA, the negative g's caused the water to shoot out of the water bottle nozzle and accumulate at the top of the canopy. Upon seeing the stream of water, Peedawg began giggling. We engineers in the control room had no clue what was going on, all we heard was the giggling. This was a high risk test mission, what the hell was there to giggle about, we wondered.

The water would slowly migrate to the rear of the canopy, ending up directly over Peedawg's head. When the maneuver was over, Flood pulled back on the stick to regain positive g's, and all that accumulated water had to go somewhere. And in this case, *somewhere* meant dropping down all over Peedawg. At that point the giggling changed to chuckling.

There were multiple negative g excursions required during that mission, and each time that poorly sealed water bottle would do its job. Giggling and chuckling were soon replaced with boisterous laughter. It was a damn funny high risk mission, and we had the whole thing on tape...

One nice thing about being an engineer versus a pilot is when I make a mistake, I am typically the only person who knows it. But when a test pilot makes a mistake, it's typically there on instrumentation or video for all to see, and to be forever saved in perpetuity. Hard data and/or video/audio tape evidence are an engineer's way of saying, "Hey look at me, I'm *not* making mistakes and you *are.*"

CHAPTER 13
IN THE BEGINNING...

My mind has a tendency to wander. No surprise there by now, I suppose.

So, I was sitting in church... Yeah, I know – Ron in church? Ha. Well, at home I pretty much do what I'm told, while on remote flight test assignments, in contrast, I'm free to be the heathen people know so well. Anyway, I digress. Sitting in church and not paying much attention, as is typical for me. When I was a kid I would draw airplanes on the church bulletin rather than listen to the preacher. Today, there would be trouble if caught drawing airplanes on church bulletins (even though it's what I really *want* to do). Instead I just *think* about them – to myself, mind you, not bothering a soul.

I'm sure some people would say, "Wow Ron, that's sad, really sad. Time you should be spending with the Lord is spent thinking about vertical tails and directional stability. You're probably going to Hell for this." No worries mate, that box has already been checked.

You see, when I was ten years old I wanted a BB gun. I asked my mother. She said "No, you'll put an eye out." [NSVMR] So I did what any ten year old boy would do – went and asked my father. I argued since he was planning to take me hunting when I got a bit older, this would be good training. He replied, "Excellent idea son. I'm glad to see one of my three children has the ability for cognitive thought." Thanks Dad. I smiled and started to walk off, but he stopped me and said, "No shooting birds." OK, no problem.

[Author's note: Ten year olds don't understand the implications and ramifications of Mom saying one thing, Dad saying another, and child choosing to listen to whichever suits his/her desires. Now having three kids of my own (each with an intermittent capacity for cognitive thought), I fully see this, in painful clarity. I'm convinced having children is God's way of paying you back for being a child once.]

Wanting a BB gun and having the means to purchase a BB gun were two different matters. But I, the child with cognitive thought capability, had already figured that one out. Mom and Dad gave me 55 cents a day to buy a school lunch plus a milk. Needing cash but not being old enough for a job, I skipped lunch and/or milk most days and pocketed the cash. (This lack of nutrition during my formative years probably explains a lot about me now.) Anyway, in the early 1970s it didn't take a lot of 55 cent cash days to amass the sum required to buy a BB gun. So, essentially no sooner than Dad said yes, and we're off to the store to buy said weapon (note background checks were not required in those footloose, carefree days).

It was a beauty. Actually it was a Daisy. Not the classic Red Ryder with a real wood stock and the leather tang mind you, but that was OK by me. My dad had been a captain in the Air Force, and well, kids of Air Force pilots just learned to make do with less. I was out in the back yard shooting at paper taped to cardboard boxes with target circles drawn on them (we were too poor to afford them fancy store-bought printed targets), and well, a kid gets kind of bored just putting holes in stationary stationery. My mind naturally wandered to thoughts of other potential targets. Being the youngest and smallest of the three children dictated that my brother and sister were not viable targets (common sense rules of engagement here). Then it appeared, as if almost on queue – a bird sitting on the peak of the garage roof, chirping merrily. I looked around (nobody watching), I raised my weapon, I held my breath, I aimed, and then I did what any red-haired, red-blooded, freckled American kid would do. I pulled the trigger.

Nice shot. No, a damn fine shot. A shot to be proud of. But as I retrieved my quarry, and held its now limp body in my hands, my pride turned to guilt and shame. That little bird was so beautiful, so very beautiful. I did not cry. I did NOT cry (as far as you know). In the annals of Phillips' family lore, this became known as the *Little Ronnie – Dead Bird Affair*. [VMR]

My fate was sealed. I stole from my parents, lied to my father, and killed an innocent creature. My passport to Heaven was revoked. My passage to Hell was confirmed. I've learned many life lessons, and one is you can't change the past, nor can you run from it – another credo, I suppose. Don't bother weeping for me. I brought this on myself, and I will deal with it. My only request is I not go to Hell alone. After working with pilots for so long, I'm pretty confident that won't be a concern. In fact, when my time comes to stroll the corridors of Hell, I fully expect to see a wing dedicated to test pilots...

I digress yet again.

So, there I was, sitting in church, and the priest was talking about the book of Genesis and the topic of creation. Which, naturally of course, got my mind to wandering about airplanes, and then to flight testing, and then to engineers, and not so naturally to pilots/WSOs. The Bible has its many versions and translations, the priest had his own interpretation, so here is my light-hearted go at it. What if, instead of Adam and Eve in the Garden of Eden... what if instead it was Pilot and WSO?

The Creation: An Engineer's Tale

In the beginning, God created the heavens and the earth. And He saw that it was good. Then God created the waters and the sky, and said, "Let the water teem with living creatures, and let birds fly above the earth." Then God said, "Let us make mankind in our image, in our likeness, so that they may rule over the fish in the sea and the birds in the sky, and over all the creatures that move along the ground." So, God created *Man*. And the first man was named *Pilot* (not to be confused with Pontius Pilot, who comes later in history). Note God originally wanted to name the new creature *Aviator*, but decided that was too many syllables for such a rudimentary beast.

So, there is Pilot, hanging around Eden, getting a bit bored, when he says to God, "Dude, this Eden thing is really cool and all, but what I'd really like is to be able to soar up in the sky with the birds." So, God, seeing this as a good way for Pilot to "rule over all creatures that move" (and obviously not seeing how this was bound to go to his head) gave Pilot the ability to fly.

After a few days of soaring over this new earth, Pilot gets bored again (seeing a pattern here?) and says to God, "Dude, this flying stuff is amazing, but I don't have anybody to brag about it to." (Note the birds and flying insects had long since tired of listening to Pilot drone on and on about his aerial exploits.) Pilot continues on, "What I'd really like is a companion, you know, a drinking buddy." So, God, having already created beer, went to work on this so-called *buddy* request.

God found Himself a bit perplexed with this task. On the one hand He considered creating a creature with completely different traits as Pilot – He'd theorized making this creature possess beauty and passion and calling her *Aviatrix*. On the other hand, He also considered creating a creature with similar traits as Pilot. God, being all-knowing, came to the realization that with the personality He gave Pilot, there would be little hope of him getting along with anybody at all unlike himself. In the end, sanity prevailed, and God opted to create this *buddy* creature with similar traits.

While Pilot was sleeping one off, God reached into Pilot's cranium, extracted a handful of brain cells, and used them to create... *WSO.*

Pilot and WSO, sharing one set of brain cells among them, were immensely happy and carefree passing the days away – filled with flying, drinking, and bossing around the lesser beings. Eden AFB was truly a wonderful place to find oneself stationed.

But God was not completely at ease, for He had come to realize while He had created Pilot and WSO, they had not really turned out to be in His image, not in His likeness. So, God, seeking to correct that misgiving and also wanting to bring some semblance of dedication, purpose, and order to Eden, created *Engineer*. And God said, "Let each creature live, prosper, and further the knowledge and well-being of earth, each according to its kind." And it was so.

Ahh, a world with engineers. Order had been restored to the universe.

Soon after came aircrew proficiency requirements, instrumentation, telemetry monitoring, flight plans, flight cards, simulator sessions, review boards, pre-flight briefings, post-flight briefings, COMM plans, Flight Manuals, Op Limits, air traffic control, airspace ranges/boundaries, supersonic corridors, chase requirements, weather minimums...

God saw all that He had made, and it was very good.

Seems appropriate to end with these two jokes...

Pilots: Looking down on people since 1903.

Q. What's the difference between God and fighter pilots?
A. God doesn't think he's a fighter pilot...

CHAPTER 14
SONIC BOOMS

Wikipedia defines and characterizes a sonic boom as the following, paraphrased:

> A sonic boom is the sound associated with the shock waves created by an object traveling through the air faster than the speed of sound. When an aircraft passes through the air it creates a series of pressure waves in front of it and behind it, similar to the bow and stern waves created by a boat. These waves travel at the speed of sound, and as the speed of the object increases, the waves are forced together, or compressed, because they cannot get out of the way of each other. Eventually they merge into a single shock wave, which travels at the speed of sound. The power, or volume, of the shock wave depends on the quantity of air that is being accelerated, and thus the size and shape of the aircraft. The sound of a sonic boom depends largely on the distance between the observer and the aircraft shape producing the sonic boom.

Shock wave patterns of an X-15 free flight model at Mach 3.5. Photo courtesy of NASA.

As a side note, it may be odd, or possibly even sad, that a highly-educated aerospace engineer such as myself used Wikipedia for the definition and characteristics of a sonic boom, as opposed to either: A) my vast and inherent knowledge of all things aerodynamic, or lacking that, then B) my college text books and/or reference material.

Let's address option A first. It may very well be sad, but in my defense, there wasn't any need to know the underlying cause of sonic booms to perform my daily aerospace engineering job in an exceptional manner. With my zero sum brain, if I chose to retain information about the cause of sonic booms, then something else, say my daughter's birth date or my shoe size, would have to go. I chose my daughter over sonic booms; I can live with that. Plus, I can type "what causes sonic booms?" at the Google prompt and get a thousand options to choose from. If I type, "when is Katy's birthday?" Google gives me a blank stare. Logic prevails. My choice is correct.

[Author's note: If I really want to come clean about aerospace engineering knowledge, then I'll have to admit I'm not 100% sure what actually causes lift and drag on an airplane. But again, it just didn't matter. Wait a minute, I'm beginning to sound like a pilot. Better stop this right now. Back on point.]

Regarding option B. Yes, I do still have most of my college text books, a subset of which are related to aerodynamics, and a subset of those would likely cover the topic of sonic booms. However, those books are packed away up in the attic, and even if fetched, it would still take some time and effort to thumb through them and find the item of interest. Wikipedia, on the other hand... well... it's right here, residing on the very computer I'm using to type these words. It is so accessible, so easy. I can't possibly resist. It's like the proverbial Junior Mint in the Seinfeld episode – how could I not want one, they're refreshing!

So, did I settle and take the easy way out? Or did I use my vast intellect to weigh the two options and choose the one that would minimize time and the consumption of energy? It does, after all, take electricity to power the lights in the attic, my body does burn calories whilst climbing up into the attic, and thus even more electricity is required to power the microwave, which heats the frozen burrito, which then provides the caloric content to fuel such a trip up into the attic. Efficiency won out – no contest. Doing my part for climate change. This was really a no brainer.

My first encounter with sonic booms was while attending college at Rolla. I can remember, while a freshmen sitting through Physics class in the Electrical Engineering (EE) building, all of a sudden, without any warning, we would hear and feel the boom, and the windows would rattle loudly. Why did the windows rattle so loudly? Because the EE building was the biggest piece of crap building on campus (but not the *oldest* building on campus). Single pane glass, metal frames, no weather stripping – yeah, them bastards rattled, and how. Why Physics in the EE building? Because every engineering student had to take Physics, regardless of their major. Classrooms had to be scrounged all over the campus just to hold us all. Sardines we were.

I didn't know it at the time, but these sonic booms were coming from brand new McDonnell Douglas F-15s flying acceptance flights out of Lambert Airport in St. Louis. Part of the acceptance test flight was a speed run, which meant they had to accelerate to twice the speed of sound, or Mach 2. These F-15s would routinely take off out of St. Louis, climb up to 35,000+ feet, point southwest towards Ft. Leonard Wood (near Rolla), and light the burners for the speed run. About the time they passed over Rolla they would attain their Mach 2 *destination*, at which time they would reduce power and decelerate for the return to St. Louis. Unknown to, or at least unheard by, the pilots was the unrolling carpet of sonic booms hitting the ground under their flight path.

Once a person understands what a sonic boom is, where it is coming from, and realizes that no, they will not die from it, or be rendered incapable of producing offspring, then it's just really cool. I don't mean the regular, every day, 1960s run of the mill cool, but shit hot cool. The first few times freshmen experienced the boom, half of them probably wet themselves. But later in college, when a bunch of aero engineering upperclassmen were sitting in class, and we got interrupted by yet another sonic boom, everybody, including the professor, nodded their heads and grinned uncontrollably during that brief but spectacular pause in the lecture. It was that cool. It's an aero thing, I suppose.

After graduating college and leaving Rolla, I feared my sonic boom head nodding experiences would come to an end. As mentioned earlier, I was involved in monitoring high-speed flight test activities on the F-15 soon after college, including some Mach 2 testing. However, that monitoring took place in St. Louis, while the jet flying our test mission was laying its sonic boom waste over rural Missouri, a hundred or more miles away. Alas, no booms for me. How frustrating. I sat right there watching the strip charts and TV monitors. I could *see* the Mach number creep up. But could *hear* nothing. Quiet. Church mouse quiet. Some engineering student or Missouri farm boy got the Mach 2 sonic boom of a lifetime, and I got nothing except the sound of fan-folding paper and the sight of wiggling pens.

Luckily for me many of my future F-15 flight test programs were conducted at Edwards AFB. In the Edwards airspace ranges, there is what's called the *high altitude supersonic corridor.* It's a rectangular track 224 miles long by 15 miles wide, and it goes right over the base. So, while monitoring high-speed missions at Edwards, our test pilot dude could be directly over our heads. Boom away sir. There's not much better in life than planning a Mach 2 test point, running pre-flight simulations, writing the test card, briefing the mission, monitoring the test point, making real-time calls, and then hearing the crack of the sonic boom from *my* test point. That single event could wash away months and months of agony and frustration engineers had to put up with on a routine basis. Cathartic. The only thing missing? Yep, the rattling of the windows in that crappy EE building.

While at Edwards AFB I also witnessed the sonic booms during several Space Shuttle landings. The shuttle, re-entering the atmosphere from space, is flying at the *speed of snot* – I think somewhere in the neighborhood of Mach 20 or 30 up at altitude. Remember the Wikipedia definition said the intensity of a sonic boom is a function of the size and shape of the aircraft. Well, the space shuttle is neither small nor does it have anything resembling a svelte aerodynamic shape.

[Author's note: I just did the very thing I hate – I used the word *aerodynamic* as an adjective. I absolutely hate when car manufacturers claim their automobile is shaped to be *more aerodynamic.* Huh? Aerodynamic is not a thing an object can physically *be*. And if it cannot *be* something, then it surely cannot be *more* or *less* of it. Everything is, or can be governed by aerodynamics. When you pick up a brick and throw it, it has now become guided by aerodynamic forces, because it has air flowing around it. What they, and everybody else, mean to say is something may be more aerodynamically *efficient*, as in sleeker, less drag, etc. To correct my previous error, I shall say the space shuttle does not have an aerodynamically *efficient* shape. There, no more hate. I feel better.]

Dig further into the cause of sonic booms and you will also learn a vehicle actually has *many* shock wave sources, emanating from the many leading and trailing edge of its surfaces (as evidenced by the previous photo). With the slender shape of most high-speed fighter aircraft, there is typically one strong shock (from the nose) followed by many weaker shocks. Thus, you typically only hear one sonic boom from a fighter jet. The space shuttle, in dramatic contrast, has a blunt nose and an enormous rear end – slender and streamlined are not the words of the day here.

Combining the effects of this large size and blunt shape with the extreme Mach numbers upon reentry, you would hear a pronounced *BOOM-BOOM* when those two strong shock waves reach the ground. Impressive, to say the least. And even more so, standing outside on the ramp when the shuttle came in, as opposed to monitoring a test mission and being stuck in a windowless building. Hearing the double boom while standing on the ramp and watching the shuttle fly overhead, land on the dry lake bed, and later get towed right past our building was without a doubt one of the better of many days spent at Edwards AFB.

CHAPTER 15
A STEREOTYPICAL ENGINEER

"I am, and ever will be, a white-socks, pocket-protector, nerdy engineer, born under the second law of thermodynamics, steeped in steam tables, in love with free-body diagrams, transformed by Laplace and propelled by compressible flow." – Neil Armstrong

I suppose I was (still am?) the stereotypical engineer – introverted, no social graces, no people skills, not a people person, and all that. I already mentioned being terribly awkward around girls while in school. I did have several girls as friends or acquaintances though. Then it dawned on me why – because I was a platonic *ally*, not a romantic *threat*. Ahh. Clarity.

Ron

I used to go to parties and sit in the corner reading magazines, as my wife likes to point out to anybody who will listen. Well, not just *any* magazines, they were the latest *Aviation Week* issues. I had to stay caught up on industry news, didn't I? I don't see the problem here. Laser focus, people.

Engineer A   Engineer B

Now, as compared to a how a fighter pilot might behave at a party, sitting in the corner and reading *Aviation Week* doesn't seem so terrible, does it? Or, as a WSO might assess the situation; if a 120 pound sack of potatoes can sit in the corner and *not* interact with people, where is the need for an engineer?

Q. How do you know if there is a fighter pilot at your party?

A. He'll tell you.

Speaking of laser focus. My college education was pretty much on a single track, no deviations. The aerospace engineering degree program at UMR allowed one *free* elective. *One*, as in a *single* course, to be chosen as I wished. Go ahead, knock myself out. No holds barred. The world was my oyster. All other *electives* were used to select what topics to focus my AE degree in, i.e. aerodynamics, propulsion, structures, etc. One free elective during four years of college. Hmm. My path was set, wasn't it?

I opted to take *Tennis*. A stroke of genius (pun intended). I passed the course with an A grade, which had the added benefit of inflating my grade point average (GPA), even if just by a small margin. Honestly, was it even conceivable to *not* get an A in tennis? It was the only course in my four year degree program where I could get an A by just showing up. I needed that.

In hindsight, I understand why I may have subliminally chosen tennis as my elective. Practicing and playing singles tennis was a *lone* activity. My opponent was eighty feet away from me – much too far to have a conversation with. Verbal communications were limited to basic scoring and foul line calls: "love", "fifteen-thirty", "out", etc. It was the outdoor equivalent of sitting in the corner reading magazines, I suppose, albeit with a slightly elevated heart rate.

I consider myself to be well educated, but certainly not well rounded or well read. In college, I read *zero* books outside of those required for course work. There was simply no time for recreational reading. Plus, I still knew my mind to be a zero sum game, so reading and retaining a novel would have required me to first relinquish any attained knowledge of say, thermodynamics.

However, one literature class was required for graduation. Apparently, the Board of Curators of the University of Missouri decided having engineering students take one literature course would make us sufficiently well rounded. Or possibly it was done as a joke – hey, let's make the nerds take a literature course, ha. Whatever the reason or motivation, the course had to be taken, and passed.

I originally thought it would be best to take it at night at a local community college while working as a co-op student, and thus lighten my course load while on campus the next semester. What a mistake. I showed up for the first night at the community college and the classroom was full of stay-at-home moms who absolutely adored reading. The professor handed out the reading list for the semester and I just about keeled over. One novel each week! Was he kidding? No, apparently he was not.

Unsurprisingly, I suppose, the moms were positively *gushing* over the list of authors and titles, and many had already read most of the books on the list. Were *they* kidding? Were there actually people who read books because it was *fun*? A blanket of reality slowly settled over me. If this course was to be graded on a curve, I was doomed. I had just successfully inflated my GPA by taking tennis, I had no intention of losing that bubble to this. After that first night of literature hell, I dropped the course and decided I would take it at Rolla with other engineering students (who hopefully felt the same about reading as I did).

Back at Rolla, home of the engineer, I grimaced and signed up for my required literature course, or more specifically, Introduction to American Masterpieces I. Masterpieces *I*? As in there was more than *one*? *American* Masterpieces? As in there was something other than *American* literature? Yes to both. I had no clue. In fact, a later review of the English Courses section of my course catalog showed it was full of this stuff. Who knew? In hindsight, I wonder what it must've felt like to be an English professor at Rolla, where the majority of students were, in all likelihood, just like me. Maybe it was penance? Maybe being an English professor at an engineering school was like me having to spend an eternity in Hell with a bunch of pilots? Or at least Purgatory. Maybe one of those professors wrote a humorous book about engineers?

Convinced all that was needed was to *survive* the semester of literature, I eked out a B grade. Whew. Many thanks to all my fellow engineering student brethren for keeping the grade curve within reach. Functioning illiterates, the lot of us...

After college, I read *maybe* one book a year. Since I didn't read much, when I did actually find myself with time to read I never knew what author or title to choose. Usually my limited free reading time came when I had to travel, a captive stuck in an airport, on a plane, or in a hotel room. So, before a trip, I would have my kids recommend a good book, as they were all avid readers (and not engineers by the way).

On one particular trip to NASA Ames they recommended *The Five People You Meet in Heaven*, by Mitch Albom. Unbeknownst to me, this book was a real tear jerker. Yes, I might've figured that out by the title, but I didn't. So, there I was, sitting on the plane, stuck in the middle seat between two other people, with Mitch Albom tugging at my heart strings.

During the approach into San Francisco there was quite a bit of turbulence and the jet was getting bounced around a lot. The approach to this particular runway was over the bay, so all you saw was blue water until the moment just before touchdown. Flying so low one could see individual waves in the water, pilot fighting to hold the wings level, and me, trying in vain to hold back tears. The occupants of seats A and C were no doubt shaken a bit by the combination of the turbulence and my apparent lack of faith in a successful conclusion to the approach and landing. Thanks, kids. Nice choice.

CHAPTER 16
PROPER USE OF TECHNOLOGY

"It has become appallingly obvious that our technology has exceeded our humanity."
— Albert Einstein

One evening while sitting in the living room with most of my family unit (wife plus two kids, first kid had been banished to study abroad in China) we debated whether technology actually brings people together or has the opposite effect. To put things in a bit of perspective, there were four of us sitting in a room with two laptops, three iPads, three iPods, four smart phones, and two cats (not iCats or e-Cats, just regular cats). On top of that there was JazzRadio.com playing wirelessly on the Sonos. There was more surfing, texting, FaceBook-ing, WeChat-ting, Tweeting, Tumblr-ing, Skype-ing, Solitaire-ing, and e-mailing going on in that room than you could shake an e-stick at. I swear, at times you could even hear the whir of electrons zinging around the house Wi-Fi zone.

So, does all this technology bring us together? You could argue all of this internet and cell-based connectivity allows for many ways to communicate with friends and family. However, take my living room example where four people were sitting in the same room, yet all four were face down in their personal technology, not speaking to each other at all. More examples? When you watch a baseball game on TV, what are more than half of the people behind home plate doing? Yep, face down, thumbs on their smart phones. Same thing at hockey games or concerts. Why spend that kind of money for a seat at a game or event just to look at your phone?

Back to my living room. I, as guilty as the rest of my family, sat on my favorite chair with an iPad on my lap. Cat #2, the one I can tolerate, sat on the floor looking up longingly at me (I don't get this from humans too much). Cat #2 continued to wait patiently. I finally noticed. I looked back to my iPad, felt a pang of guilt, and then opted to put the iPad aside and invited the cat to my lap. Cat #2 won; technology lost. Cat #1, whose sole purpose in life is to annoy me, was busy licking herself in unmentionable places, no relevance to this story at all.

"I like pigs. Dogs look up to us. Cats look down on us. Pigs treat us as equals."
— Winston Churchill

[Author's note: Although I mention my cats sporadically, this is decidedly *not* a cat book, and I am decidedly *not* a cat author. In fact, I'm more of a dog person, but that's a different topic. If you do want to read a good cat book, I highly recommend *Dumb Bunnies and Expecting Cats* by Matthew Moen.]

That evening, I insisted the family all play some form of non-electronic game together (yes, my kids both love me and hate me at the same time). They decided on *Hearts*.

Excellent. This was a *real* game. It required a *physical* deck of cards, shuffling, and dealing, i.e. manual dexterity. In addition, I am a self-proclaimed master at *Hearts*. I never lose. We play. I lost – badly. There was much rejoicing among the remaining family members. (You must understand that pummeling their father in *Hearts* would be on par with USA beating Germany 4-0 in World Cup soccer.)

Later, my wife suggested the two of us play *Cribbage*. Excellent. I am a self-proclaimed master at *Cribbage*. I never lose. We play. I lost – badly. More rejoicing. So much for non-electronic games. I retreated to e-*Solitaire* on my iPad (at least when I lose there is no e-rejoicing).

So, there we were, full circle, back to the living room, four souls with heads down into their personal technology. I glanced up and saw kid #3 grinning. I asked him what was so funny. He read me a Tumblr thread...

Thread #1: *The sun has come out.*
Thread #2: *The sun is so gay.*
Thread #3: *Why are all the hot ones gay?*

Cracked me up. I came to the conclusion that *humor* is the proper use of technology. Below is another excerpt of good technology...

> An elderly couple had just learned how to send text messages on their cell phones. The wife was a romantic type, and the husband was more of a no-nonsense guy.
>
> One afternoon, the wife went out to meet a friend for coffee. She decided to send her husband a romantic text message, and she wrote: "If you are sleeping, send me your dreams. If you are laughing, send me your smile. If you are eating, send me a bite. If you are drinking, send me a sip. If you are crying, send me your tears. I love you."
>
> After a long pause, the husband texted back to her: "I'm on the toilet. Please advise."

While it's hard to argue technology hasn't brought many improvements, at times I miss working back in the old days. Remote assignment flight testing back in the 1980s just seemed more fun. There was no internet, no e-mail, no instant messaging, and no cell phones. While at Edwards AFB, I was essentially isolated, on my own, a lone cowboy in a sea of fast jets. (That last part was a feeble attempt to add glory, just in case somebody decides they want to make a movie from this book. Think engineering version of *Top Gun*.)

While working at Edwards AFB, the only connection with your boss or wife (your *other* boss) was the phone on your desk. Caller ID didn't exist back then, so when the phone rang we would just sit there and stare at it, too afraid to talk to either our boss or our wife. We knew if it was truly important, they would leave a message with the secretary, and then we could call back, presumably at our leisure. (Note: *At our leisure* was code-speak for *after mustering up the courage*.)

One funny part was hearing a *different* phone ring and turning to look at some other engineer, that same deer in the headlights stare, too afraid to pick up his phone as well. Poor bastard. The only people who *did* pick up their phones were the single guys who were sucking up to their bosses, trying to get promoted.

The other funny part was seeing some dude not answer his phone, hearing it transfer over to the secretary, and seeing the disgusted look on her face while scribing the message, all while that dude sat at his desk in full view of her. One time we had a secretary who simply wouldn't put up with any crap from engineers, and would yell, "Hey shithead, I see you, answer your damn phone!" at the offending engineer, loud enough so all could hear. Funny stuff – well, funny if it wasn't you being the shithead, I suppose.

Thirty years later, I found myself again 1800 miles away from home at Palmdale on a *remote* assignment. However, due to the wonder of computers, the internet, instant messaging (IM), and that little IM status window, my wife, who also worked at Boeing back home in St. Louis, knew the exact moment I got up from my desk to go pee and the exact moment I returned. Technology sucked. And when my wife called my desk, sent me a text or IM, and I didn't respond, but then she saw my IM status was *available*, well then I had some explaining to do, didn't I. The modern day equivalent of "Hey shithead, I see you, answer your damn phone!" I suppose.

"We live in a society exquisitely dependent on science and technology, in which hardly anyone knows anything about science and technology." – Carl Sagan

CHAPTER 17
FLIGHT TEST EQUIPMENT?

I went to the doctor for a routine physical and he told me since I was over 50, it was time for the big C. Yep, Colonoscopy. My wife heard the news. She was ecstatic. How could that be? How could the mere thought of my potential future pain and embarrassment bring such joy to another person? And not just any person, but the person who had vowed to stick with me in good times and bad, in sickness and in health? More on that later...

I must confess, I was actually a bit over 51 when that little meeting with the doc occurred. So, as you might surmise, the wife had been on my case about this for quite a while – giving me gentle reminders, not so gentle reminders, agitated reminders. If a stranger off the street treated you like this, you'd go to court and get a restraining order. But when your wife does it, it's called *love*. Boy, I never felt more *loved*.

A few days before the *procedure*, we sat down at the dinner table and tried to explain to child #3 what this colonoscopy thing was all about. Side note: kids #1 and #2 evidently saw this day coming and had long since bailed out of the home, under the guise of, "Gotta go to college, see ya Dad." So, there I was trying to tell kid #3 as delicately as possible what is involved in the procedure and the prep. Wife, who had a huge grin on her face, could almost not control her overflowing joy. I didn't get it. Finally, I just stopped, and summarized for kid #3, "All you need to know about my impending colonoscopy is it involves a big hose, my rectum, and a video camera, and the three words that keep coming from your mother's mouth are *fun* and *so happy*."

The day before arrives. I had to mix an entire bottle of MiraLax with a half-gallon of Gatorade and drink it. For those who might be new to the topic of rectal flushing sports, MiraLax is technically a *stool softener*. Oh hell yeah. Especially when you consume the entire bottle in one sitting. I spent the next twelve hours or so coming and going, so to speak. It wasn't *fun*, and I wasn't *so happy*, as previously advertised. I sat on the couch in the basement (ten feet from the bathroom), pulled the blanket over me, turned the TV on, and prepared for a *fun* evening.

Hard to believe, but the most annoyed living creature in my house was cat #1. Side note: cat #2 must've also seen this day coming and decided to avoid any and all contact with me. Cat #1 saw the blanket and thought warm, cozy thoughts of snuggling with her master. Master? Yeah right. Anyway, cat #1 hopped up and nestled in tight. Ten minutes went by, then it was move the cat, move the blanket, get up, squirt-wipe-flush, back on couch (in that order, do not confuse that). Cat #1 looked mildly annoyed. After several hours of this routine, cat #1 was starting to get pissed. At one point during yet another move-move-stand-sit-squirt-wipe-flush-stand-sit routine, cat #1 gave me the evil eye and a long growl-like meow. So sorry to inconvenience you, dear cat. At that point the little devil in us all appeared to me and said, "Do it, go put some MiraLax in the cat's water bowl." Then the little practical engineer in us all appeared and said, "Are you nuts?

That cat craps in a small box located in *your* house. You really want that cat to have loose stool?" Sanity prevailed. Cat's stool remained solid. Engineer 1. Devil 0.

The next morning mercifully arrives – the day of the procedure, which was preceded by, yes, an enema (is there really anything left up there?). I pulled the bottle from the box, and read the instructions. There was a large orange cap covering the business end of the bottle. My first thought? All flight test equipment is painted orange. Enemas, therefore, must be flight test equipment. No idea why I thought that. It was 7 o'clock in the morning, and I had just spent an entire night with fitful bouts of sleep interrupting my now routine sit-squirt-wipe-flush cycle. I was barely coherent.

Anyway, the instructions had a warning written in bold caps REMOVE ORANGE COVER PRIOR TO INSERTION. Really? Was this something that could possibly be confused? Wow. I thought maybe there should be one of those REMOVE BEFORE FLIGHT banners hanging from the orange cap. There's another lesser warning (I'll call it a *Caution*, like in the Flight Manual, as opposed to a *Note*) that said to insert it in the proper orientation. Really? Like somebody's gonna stick the large bulb end of the bottle in first? Good heavens. Lowest common denominator, I suppose. Anyway, process completed – and yes, Ron, there was *more* up there.

We arrived at the surgery center and, after signing my life away on a multitude of forms, they prepped me – on the rolling bed, IV hooked up with saline solution, blood pressure monitor, pulse Ox monitor, etc. They invited the wife to come back to sit with me until T-minus five. Yep, she was still smiling. Glad to oblige. After a few minutes of small talk, we found ourselves out of topics, so she began staring at my vital signs on the monitor. She instructed me to calm down; my heart rate was at 95. A few minutes passed by, and she reiterated, you really need to relax, it's now up to 97. Another minute or two passed, then it was at 100, and she became quite insistent. In a sudden stroke of genius, she realized she'd been looking at the pulse Ox monitor number, not the heart rate. All this time my pulse Ox was near 100% (good) and my heart rate was in the low 70s (also good, considering the impending doom about to befall me).

To be entirely honest, I probably deserved that. During the birth of child #1, when she was hooked up to all the monitors and the strip chart was running, what was I doing? Yep, monitoring that strip chart data (I'm an engineer, it's what I do). Along comes another contraction, but this time it's a biggie – the strip chart pen goes off-scale. I turned to her and said, "I bet that one hurt, huh?" I'm fairly certain her thoughts at that moment were something along the lines of "I'll get you, you SOB." Well, it took 20 years and 9 months, but mission accomplished.

Speaking of childbirth, here's another joke...
Q. *What do fighter pilots use for birth control?*
A. *Their personality.*

The rest of the day was easy. The actual procedure was a non-event, mainly because I slept through it (in no way interested in seeing what *instruments* would be used, the less known the better). Whatever that anesthesiologist gave me, I'm buying it. Wonderful.

Best 45 minute nap I'd ever taken. Clean as a whistle, thank you for asking. Wife told kid #3 this was the only time in my life I was not full of shit. He found the humor, but also felt my pain.

[Author's note: Author and columnist Dave Barry wrote a humorous description of his colonoscopy experience as well, which I read after writing about my experience. I highly recommend reading his story.]

It's probably sad that my first lucid thought after that fitful night was *flight test equipment* – something definitely work related. I suppose that's just to be expected after one has spent so many years working in the same industry. I have been amazed at times what was in, or not in, my zero sum mind at any given moment. For example, if I were asked how old my kids were, or their birth dates, I would have to pause and think (or count). Conversely, if I were asked what table in the F-15 aero database was yawing moment due to rudder, I would reply without hesitation (that table is *ATAB68* by the way). Such is life.

CHAPTER 18
FRESH

I suppose if I feel comfortable enough writing about my colonoscopy, then this next story should not be a problem for me. Either that or I simply have no shame.

Back in the early 90s my wife and I decided it was time to start having kids. To be honest, it was my wife who decided it was time; I was just along for the ride. Kind of like on a weekend when she would ask me, "Hey, do you want pizza for dinner?" and I would reply, "Umm... sure." Kids? Umm... sure. How hard could it be?

No luck. We had all the requisite parts and all the requisite procedural knowledge. Yes, I said I was awkward and shy around women, but I was not a moron.

And here is where it gets a little awkward. To quote Matthew Moen from *Dumb Bunnies and Expecting Cats*, "Midwestern boys are taught early on, or else are wise enough to figure out all on their own, that it is generally quite rude to discuss female gynecological issues over the telephone, especially with total strangers." Midwestern boy? Check. Total strangers? Check.

Suffice it to say that health insurance companies would not even touch fertility issues until *after* the father was ruled out as a potential problem. Wow, putting the man *before* the woman, that was a new concept for me, and to be honest I actually felt a little special. That special feeling was not to last long.

Off to the urologist office I went. Apparently, they needed a *sample* from me. I had no clue. Two things were important here – count and motility. Again, no clue. Was *motility* even a word? No need to actually see the urologist; I just needed to stop by the reception desk and pick up the required *tools*. In this case, the only *tool* necessary was a sample cup – everything else was up to me. This would be an out-patient procedure, as it were.

I walked through the waiting room up to the desk and announced my name. The nurse asks me what I was there for. Really? I had an appointment. They knew I was coming, right? That is what it means to have an *appointment*? Did I really have to say it out loud? I repeated my name and mentioned, again, that I had an appointment. She was neither satisfied nor amused. Apparently, working as a nurse at an urologist office was not a primo gig, and no doubt she likely got grief and attitude from both the patients and the doctors. She was having none of it from me that morning.

The nurse asked again what I was there for. I mumbled a possibly inaudible, "sperm sample." She said, "What?" Did I mention the waiting room was full of people? OK, Ron, nothing else to do but man up. I repeat, "sperm sample" at an entirely audible volume, with possibly just a hint of indignation. I instantly felt the daggers from multiple sets of eyes in the waiting room piercing my back, but did not dare turn around. If being proverbially shot was to be my fate, well then they were just going to have to proverbially shoot me in the back. Cowards. All of them.

The nurse is now fully in the know. Yeah right. She *knew*. She knew what I was there for. She knows what *every* patient is there for. But she takes some sort of vindictive delight in seeing grown men squirm. Am I right? But here's the kicker – there was no grin, no apparent pleasure for her. If I did that to somebody, I'd at least find the humor in it – I'd likely be grinning from ear to ear. But not her. This was not about humor. She was a man-hater, a vicious breed. I'd heard about them before. This is why you watched channels like *Animal Planet* – to be prepared for times like these. Bear encounter in the woods? Got it. Rattlesnake in the desert? Got it. Crocodile in the river? Got it. Man-hater nurse at the front desk? Check. A Boy Scout is *prepared*. Give me your best shot, I am ready. No, as it turned out, I wasn't.

She hands me the sample cup along with the instruction sheet. Instructions? Really? I'd been taking care of myself, as it were, for years, didn't really see the need for instructions in this matter. Could it get worse? Yes. Man-hater nurse then proceeded to *read* the instructions aloud, ostensibly for all in the waiting room to hear. Was this really required? Sure, I was a functioning illiterate engineer, but I *could* read (she was obviously not aware I got a B in American Masterpieces I). But there I was, standing in front of the waiting room firing squad, with details of my future miscreant behavior being read aloud to me by my nurse executioner. Daggers. Daggers I say.

She left me with a single parting shot, "Do you have any questions?" What sane man would *dare* ask a question at that point? No man, sane or otherwise. Not a peep from me. And she knew that as well. Maximum effect. It's a vicious and *calculating* breed.

I took the only option open to me. I grabbed the sample cup and the instruction sheet, turned around, and walked as briskly as possible out of the waiting room, avoiding any and all eye contact. I got to my car and just sat there, speechless, motionless, needing to decompress. Apparently, kids were going to be more difficult than I had imagined, and I had no clue the difficulty would start before they even arrived on scene. I started the car and drove to work. Even a stressful day of engineering would be a cakewalk compared to what I had just endured – there was some comfort in that.

The next morning – the day of the procedure, as it were, I read the instructions and took care of business. The only two things of note in the instructions were that the sample needs to be *collected* relatively recently and also kept warm. My only concern here was it was the middle of winter with a 15 minute drive to the urologist's office. No problem. I'm an engineer. I solve problems. It's what I do. I took the no longer empty sample cup, tightened the lid, tucked it inside my shirt, put my coat on, and headed out to the office. I was dreading this. It was one thing to walk out of an office with an *empty* sample cup, it was an entirely different thing to walk into an office with a *full* sample cup, at least in my mind. And there was no *Animal Planet* episode that covered this situation as far as I knew.

My worst fears did *not* materialize. The waiting room was empty. The man-hater nurse executioner was nowhere to be seen. I walked up to the desk and placed the sample cup on the counter. The lovely nurse at the desk knew *exactly* what was going on. My name was on the pre-printed label affixed to the cup. She asked me not a single thing. I was required to speak not a single word. She smiled and simply said, "Thanks." I left. What a pleasant experience. My faith in humanity was restored. (Note, I even considered dropping our cable TV.)

If this story were to end right here, it would have been humorous enough (well, *after* the fact) and potentially worth writing about. Does this story end here? No. Oh hell no.

In a few days I got a call from the urologist's office with the results: sperm count was fine, but motility was low. *Motility*, as I learned, was the amount of movement or motion exhibited by the little fellas. I had plenty of the little fellas; they just weren't as active as the doctor would have liked. I hope that wasn't too graphic for you. Anyway, the urologist requested a second sample. Apparently, motility can be very sensitive to the age of the sample, and the urologist would like a second sample just be sure.

A bit dejected? Yes. But I was *fully* committed to this having kids thing. Kids? "Umm... sure?" Yeah, I'm all in. Plus, I'm an engineer – I understood the concept of *redundancy*. I understood the desire for a second set of data before irrevocably labeling a man with the social stigma, the curse of *low motility*. I had already spent half a lifetime dealing with being a short, slow, myopic dog paddler. God had told me in no uncertain terms that I could not be an aviator, was He now telling me I could not be a father? Was I one of those people joked about who should not be allowed to procreate?

Keep your focus, Ron. OK, off to the urologist's office for a *third* time. My worst fears reappear. The waiting room was full. Man-hater nurse executioner was holding court at the reception desk. Oh well, I had a job to do. This was no time for passivity. I proceeded directly to the desk. I didn't wait for her to ask, I told her my name and what I was there for. I had learned my lesson.

She recognized me. She was waiting for me. She *knew*. She *knew* my first sample came back with low motility. She *knew* a stale sample could have a big impact on motility. She handed me the cup and another copy of the instruction sheet. I did not allow her to read the instructions aloud again. I immediately turned and started to walk past the reassembled firing squad. But, as I soon learned, this was *not* the end of that encounter. I was about half-way through the waiting room when man-hater nurse executioner yelled my name, "Mister Phillips!" I stopped and turned around. "It needs to be *FRESH*."

Well, if there was any doubt whatsoever about why I was at the urologist's office that day, it was now forever erased. Everybody, and I mean *everybody*, in the waiting room and the rest of the office now knew exactly what I was there for. Clarity. Crystal.

There would not be any more humiliation. Read my lips, there will *not* be a *third* sample required. Being a man of documented low motility, I did not dare risk a possible stale sample by driving home, collecting the sample, and driving back to the office. No. I waltzed out of the waiting room and headed to the nearest restroom, strategically located just down the hall. I manned up and did my duty. I was not particularly proud of this act, but to be honest pride had nothing to do with it anymore. It was personal. Maybe it shouldn't have been? Maybe I was over-reacting? Maybe. Possibly. Pride and logic are sometimes diametrically opposed. Emotions aside, I still had a job to do.

Having manned up successfully, I sealed the cup, and left the restroom. I immediately walked right back into the office and strolled past the waiting room firing squad. The firing squad members were still talking in hushed voices about what had transpired just moments before. I stopped at the reception desk. No more than two or three minutes had elapsed since I had left the office, empty cup in hand. Man-hater nurse executioner was still sitting there. Excellent. I slammed the now 98 deg F sample cup down on the counter and proclaimed, "It's FRESH!"

The stunned look on her face, and on the others in the office, was priceless. That chatty nurse who could recite sperm sample instructions verbatim was now speechless. Without another word spoken, I turned and walked out of the office.

In a couple of days I got another call from the urologist's office: count fine, motility excellent. Damn straight. Confirmed – I had the ability to pass on my short, slow, myopic, dog paddler, small bladder, nerd genes to future generations...

CHAPTER 19
THERE AND BACK AGAIN...

"Engineering is the art of modelling materials we do not wholly understand, into shapes we cannot precisely analyze, so as to withstand forces we cannot properly assess, in such a way that the public has no reason to suspect the extent of our ignorance."
– Dr. AR Dykes

Enough about my personal life and medical procedures, back to engineering...

What I liked most about my engineering job was I got to see a multitude of projects from start to finish. Whenever we sold F-15s to a new customer, added some new store capability, or expanded some portion of the envelope, I was typically a part of the process from early initial development to the final implementation.

For the potential new customers, I was involved in the initial proposal writing – describing the aerodynamic, flight controls, and performance aspects of the F-15 – in other words putting down into text and charts how the jet flies, how the jet performs, and why they *want* this jet, why they *need* this jet. After the contractor proposals were submitted, the competition phase came, where my involvement usually consisted of briefing the potential customers about the characteristics mentioned in the proposal and supporting simulation demo sessions.

Variants of the F-15E Strike Eagle won the competitions for Israel, Saudi Arabia (twice), South Korea (twice), and Singapore. After winning it was our (aero) job to clear any new stores, pods, etc. the customer wanted and to define the allowable flight envelopes. This typically involved wind tunnel testing (including on-site monitoring of the test at the tunnel facility), building increments for the aerodynamic database, and then running 6-DOF analyses for the new stores. In some cases, flight testing was also required, which included all of the TIS and TRB/SRB activities mentioned earlier, plus that most dreaded of tasks – working with test pilots. Ha...

I was also involved in teaching courses to the foreign customer engineers and/or pilots. The primary topics typically included aerodynamics, flight controls, flying qualities, high AOA flight, departures, spins, etc. Volumes could be written about all of the interactions with foreign customers, but I'll keep it to a few short stories or characteristics.

We had Korean engineers in St. Louis for a six month long course. I was not the primary instructor, but taught a few select topics. My overall impression of the Korean engineers was that they were generally inquisitive, but seemed a bit more interested in having an opportunity to live in the United States than they were with the actual course material. Funny, the one thing an instructor could absolutely *not* do was interrupt their morning and afternoon smoke breaks.

Israeli engineers were in St. Louis for several months, and we taught them about F-15 aerodynamics and flight controls. The Israelis would ask a *ton* of questions. They would also request *volumes* of test data, reports, and artifacts, even though they knew full well we were not allowed to provide them, per USG releasability rules. They would ask. We would politely decline. They would ask the next day, or ask the next instructor, for exactly the same information. The answer never changed. It grew tiresome.

Two Saudi Air Force engineers came to St. Louis for about a week-long course. Their commander, a lieutenant colonel I believe, was with them. The two engineers were inquisitive – they *wanted* to ask questions. Their commander, however, had a different plan. He was just interested in getting through the day in the shortest possible time. At first, when one of the engineers would ask a question, or ask for clarification, the lieutenant colonel would roll his eyes or shake his head. Later, he would actually cut them off in mid-sentence, not allowing them to ask the question. Chain of command, I suppose. Higher rank won. Questions squelched. Too bad.

Singapore sent a group of about twenty engineers and pilots for a several week course. What a great group of people. They were attentive, inquisitive, and intelligent. It was obvious they wanted to be there and wanted to learn. One of the engineers asked so many questions that soon I had to cut her off or we'd never make it through all of the material. After that I gave her a strict daily quota for questions – she had to learn to live within her means.

In addition to all of the analysis and teaching, I supported the production and assembly of the jets in the factory. If any parts didn't come together properly and it impacted the outer moldline (OML) of the jet, then an aero engineer was called in to accept or reject the parts. We were also called in to troubleshoot jets that had aero or flight controls issues/anomalies discovered during the acceptance test flights (yes, more pilots).

In the end, seeing a Singapore jet, for example, take off from Lambert Airport gave me a great deal of pride. Pride in knowing the jet was being flown with new items I cleared to fly, and flown per the Flight Manual limits (hopefully) I analyzed and wrote. Pride in knowing that, years earlier, I was there helping to write the initial proposal that started the competition. Writing that proposal was a pain in the ass, yet another distraction I didn't have time for. But years later seeing those jets roll off the line and get airborne made it worthwhile. Many people at Boeing would work on nothing but proposals – as soon as one was written they would move to the next proposal. I couldn't do that. OK, in reality, I *wouldn't* do that. I wanted to be there at each step. I wanted to see the *final* product.

One of the more memorable start-to-finish projects I worked on was the IRST for the Koreans. You may remember I mentioned in an earlier chapter we flew the IRST on F-15E#1 to collect aerodynamic data – when Dragon grudgingly did that Mach 1.8 CAS off *thingy.*

The first issue to deal with was where on the jet to mount the IRST. It's not always easy putting a new sensor on the F-15, given that installing it was probably never even imagined back in the late 1960s when the F-15 was originally designed. Every location considered had its own long list of drawbacks. Since the IRST needed to look ahead (i.e. needed a field of view forward, up/down, and side/side), locating it really tied our hands. In the end, we opted to incorporate the IRST into the Target Pod pylon, located underneath the left engine inlet.

Having a design concept and location in mind, off we went to the wind tunnel. Actually *off we went* is a huge understatement of the prep work required to test in a wind tunnel. Just like in flight test, there is a TIS to write/approve, a review process, and model parts to design and fabricate – in total about a year long process. At least with wind tunnel testing, there were no pilots to deal with – whew.

After the wind tunnel test was completed (at Arnold AFB in Tullahoma, TN), we used that tunnel data to develop the aerodynamic increments required for the 6-DOF and performance computer models. After running high speed 6-DOF simulations we learned the jet would not be able to fly to the maximum speeds desired by the customer. The IRST, mounted under the left inlet, introduced an aerodynamic yaw asymmetry that needed to be balanced by the rudders. The problem was the rudders were inherently limited in deflection capability due to the high speeds (referred to as hinge moment limits, a typical characteristic of all high speed aircraft).

Now what? We had more meetings (it's what we in the Aerospace industry do). A few of us from engineering and program management sat at a conference table and kicked around potential solutions to the problem. The only really viable solution was to add something similar in IRST size and shape to the other side of the jet, which would effectively balance out the yaw asymmetry of the IRST alone. Voila, the IRST Adapter Shape (IAS) was born.

IAS side story... The IAS was, as its name implies, just a shape. That was its only function. So the designers had a thought – why not put a door on it, that way it could be used to carry something, i.e. become functional. Good idea. The next logical question was, how big should the door be? Alas, the IAS was not large enough to carry golf clubs. I knew it was, however, large enough to carry beer. So I posed the question, "Well, how big is a case of beer?" It was final. No more discussion. The door would be sized to fit a case of beer.

OK, back to aero analysis... We used Computational Fluid Dynamics (CFD) computer solutions to help validate the IAS would effectively balance out the IRST. Then it was back to the wind tunnel (yeah, I know, write the TIS, design/fab the parts, conduct the test, analyze the data, develop increments). The wind tunnel confirmed the CFD results, i.e. that the IRST and IAS combination generated little to no yaw asymmetry. Success! Partially.

CFD is nice (sometimes) and wind tunnel data is nice (sometimes). But what we really needed in order to prove safety of flight was actual flight data. So, off we went to flight test (mentioned in an earlier chapter). Long story short – the IAS worked as expected. In the Flight Manual one will see airspeed limits for the IRST and/or IAS, and customers are flying to those limits today (if they actually read them).

So, from the humble beginnings of a bunch of engineers sitting around a conference table debating IRST where and how, we went from initial concept development to final implementation. I was involved in each step along the way. I debated each pro/con. I planned and monitored two wind tunnel tests. I developed increments for the aerodynamic database. I ran the 6-DOF analysis. I planned the flight testing. I spent a week at Eglin AFB monitoring the test flights. I analyzed the flight data and updated the aerodynamic database. I reran the 6-DOF analysis. I wrote the Flight Manual limits. Now, I can do a Google search and find photos of F-15s flying with the IRST. It's hard to beat that.

[Author's note: Don't take this last paragraph the wrong way. I don't mean to use "I did..." in the sense that I was some great engineer or that only I could have done this. Neither are the case. The IRST just happened to be the project assigned to me. While I was working the IRST the other aero engineers in my group were busy working on their assigned projects.]

Many engineers from *other* disciplines (not aero) also worked on the IRST, but most were only involved in their specific discipline. For example, the wind tunnel engineers only worked on the IRST during the wind tunnel test portion. They saw neither the tradeoffs during the initial design concept phase nor the flight testing that followed. The flight test engineers saw the flight test portion, but not the design/analysis leading up to or following the actual testing. Not that this is bad. Those engineers got to see, in effect, a shorter window of time for a bunch of different projects, which is no doubt one of the things they liked about their jobs.

I, on the other hand, preferred being a part of *every* phase of a *single* project, seeing each step along the way, all the way to completion. It takes both kinds of engineers. We're a village – quite possibly a village of functioning illiterate engineers, but a village nonetheless.

OK, enough of the boring, nerd engineer speak...

CHAPTER 20
LIFE IN THE DEFENSE/AEROSPACE INDUSTRY

I wanted to discuss what it was like working in this industry. Then I found this old email. Seems like a great way to start off. Sure, you could change a word or two to bring it up to the current decade, but overall it's pretty realistic.

You might be in the Defense/Aerospace Industry if...

1. *You sat at the same desk for 4 years and worked for 8 different managers. Or have moved 5 times in two years and have never known who your boss was.*
2. *You get really excited about a 3% pay increase.*
3. *You sit in a cubicle smaller than your bedroom closet.*
4. *Its dark on your drive to and from work.*
5. *Fun is when projects are assigned to someone else.*
6. *Communication is something your group is having problems with.*
7. *You see a good-looking person and know it's a visitor.*
8. *Free food left over from a meeting is your main staple.*
9. *All art involves a white board.*
10. *All real work is done prior to 8:00 AM and after 4:30 PM.*
11. *You're already late on the assignment you just received.*
12. *Dilbert is your favorite cartoon.*
13. *Your boss's favorite lines are:*
    "When you get a few minutes..."
    "I have an opportunity for you..."
    "Cross-charging is forbidden."
    "We have a new culture that will enable us to..."
    "This reorganization will allow us to streamline our way of doing business, of becoming more competitive."
14. *99% of the people in your company do not know what you do.*
15. *99% of the people in your company do not care what you do.*
16. *Vacation is something you rollover to next year.*
17. *Everyone at the company says that without their work there would be no aircraft.*
18. *An ordinary secretary has more power than an old engineer.*
19. *You read this entire list and understand it.*

I'm actually not laughing, I'm crying.

It's a pretty comprehensive list, to be sure. But I would add to the list something along the lines of "the answer to every problem is to have more *communication*." Why is a *lack* of communication almost always cited as the root cause of a design or test problem that arises in this industry? Really? Based on what facts?

So, the obvious *fix* to any problem was to have *more* meetings, *more* phone calls, *more* status reports, etc. More meetings, in reality, just added to the *illusion* of communication and progress. Requiring more meetings and status reports just took time away from the very engineers who were trying to analyze and correct the problem with precious little schedule and resources available to them. But management felt compelled to do *something*. And since they couldn't actually solve the problem themselves, they asked more from the engineers.

OK, off my soap box.

How about this *Status Report Interpretation Guide* to end with some levity...

What it *Says* versus what it *Means*...

Schedule exposure →	Slipped 3 weeks ago
Essentially complete →	Half done
We predict →	We hope
Impact is being determined →	Anybody know where we are or what we're doing?
Task force will review →	7 people who are incompetent at their regular jobs have been loaned to the project
Not well defined →	Nobody has thought about it
Not well understood →	Now that we have thought about it, we don't want to think about it anymore
Basic agreement, but... →	The idiots won't return our calls
Results are being quantified →	We're massaging numbers to justify our conclusions
Results are encouraging →	Power-on produced no smoke
Less than expected →	Another dead end
Serious, but not insurmountable problems →	It'll take a miracle, at least
Risk is high, but acceptable →	With 10 times the budget and headcount we stand a 50/50 chance.
Aggressive milestone →	Management is dreaming again
Potential show stopper →	All team members have updated their resumes
Requires further attention →	Totally out of control
No contingency exists →	Cancel vacations, kiss the family goodbye, bring a cot and a change of underwear

CHAPTER 21
ONE OF THE FUN MISSIONS

After spending its first 20 years at Edwards AFB, F-15E#1 moved to St. Louis, where it stayed for years serving as a test platform for various programs. Since E#1 was fully instrumented, we in aero used it to flight test new pods and/or stores, and since we had a full flight test telemetry (TM) station on site, we conducted many test programs from our own buildings at St. Louis Lambert Airport.

One summer, Boeing was requested to provide a fighter to conduct a flyover for a Cardinals-Dodgers baseball game at Busch stadium. F-15E#1 was chosen. Since the schedule coincided with one of our aero test missions, we combined both into a single sortie. The flyover was to consist of a low altitude, high speed pass with a full afterburner zoom climb over the stadium, timed just as the national anthem concluded. The cool part for me was this was at the end of our normal test mission that several of us engineers were monitoring from the TM control room.

We took off around 5:30 PM, did an hour or so of my aerodynamics test points, and then headed to the staging area around 6:40. The national anthem was supposed to be sung precisely at 7:00 (timed down to the nearest 10 seconds), so our pilot, Dragon, did oval patterns over Horseshoe Lake (east of St. Louis) for 20 minutes prior to the run in.

I never realized all the coordination that went on for something like this, but Dragon was talking with us (data), our radio room, and air traffic control (KC center and STL local). Plus we had a guy at the stadium with a UHF radio giving us on-the-scene timing updates.

Finally the moment arrives. After 20 minutes or so of boring oval patterns, it seemed like all hell broke loose and there was 60 seconds of flurried activity. The stadium dude radioed, "Wrapping up God Bless America." Dragon radioed ATC for permission to step down to 2100 ft altitude (1500 ft above ground) and turned for the last oval pattern. The stadium dude radioed, "Starting national anthem." Dragon cut the last oval pattern short and turned in towards the stadium to be over the initial point at the exact prescribed time. The WSO, Snitch, called out time and distance numbers, directing Dragon when to add power and when to cut power. The stadium dude radioed, "Oh no! The national anthem will finish early." Snitch initially said, "OK, we're OK," then abruptly changed to "No! We're late! Add power. Go! Go! Go!"

Dragon accelerated toward Busch stadium in full afterburner, reached the stadium, pulled to vertical and climbed to 7,000 ft altitude while still in afterburner (thunderous vibrations enough to set off car alarms in the parking lots). Just as Dragon started the pull up, the stadium dude keyed his mike – we could hear both the engines in afterburner and the roar of the crowd. At the top of the climb Dragon rolled, pulled inverted, and leveled out. He came back to Lambert Airport, landed, taxied in, and did our final test point; flight control sweeps. Records turned off.

The Busch stadium crowd got their F–15 flyover. But that wasn't just any F–15. That was a fully instrumented F–15. The first F–15E model. That was *my* F–15. It was flying *my* mission. Not that any of that mattered to the 50,000+ in the crowd. But it mattered to me.

Some days at work were good days...

CHAPTER 22
IN MEMORIAM

I've had to deal with a few deaths while working as an engineer. Luckily not very many, but a few. I'm not special here, as everybody knows somebody who has died, but I wanted to spend a few words in reflection.

There have been a few engineers I've worked with who died at a relatively young age. To be expected when one works at a company that employs thousands of engineers – it's all built into the life expectancy statistics, I get that. In most cases, you found yourself sad for a few days or so, but then you quickly moved on. The busy routine of work and home life consumes yet again, and the memory of that person kind of fades into the background. And maybe that's the truly sad part – the memories do tend to fade. But then again there's the old saying "life is for the living"; which rings true as well. We can't have generations of people moping around all the time just because they knew somebody who died, can we? There are jobs to be done and lives to be lived. I don't have any answers here.

So, a couple of death related personal stories from me...

My first memory of seeing somebody die was a Thunderbird pilot, Maj. Joe Howard, at an airshow at Dulles Airport, Washington D.C. in June of 1972. I was ten years old. The Thunderbirds, flying F-4 Phantoms, were in the middle of their routine. They had just finished a multi-ship pass over the field, and started to pull up, all in unison. However, one of the F-4s, soon after starting the pull-up, stopped climbing, slowed, and fell towards the ground (we later learned it was a stabilator failure).

Maj. Howard was able to eject successfully, however, he descended in his chute right over the burning wreckage of his F-4. The fire consumed his chute and he died upon impact with the ground. The remaining jets flew a missing man formation over the field as a tribute, and then ended the show. Hearing about a crash, or seeing it on the news was one thing. Seeing it live was quite another, and it left a lasting impression.

We didn't know the guy, but while at Rolla we heard of a student who committed suicide, supposedly because he couldn't handle the coursework and the pressure. His father was an executive at a railroad company, and as the story goes, the father was putting immense pressure on his son to become an engineer, later to be groomed as a leader in the company. How did he choose to die? He laid on the railroad tracks near campus and waited for the train. Wow.

So, why this story, given that I neither knew him personally nor have any way to validate it? It made two thoughts sink firmly into my head. One: not everybody is cut out to be an engineer. Just being good at science and math in high school is no guarantee. And two: do not pressure your kids to become something *you* want them to be. Let them make their own choices, even if it means making their own mistakes. I don't think I could've survived being that railroad executive. And I don't want my kids to pick a career based on *my* wishes, and then later in life look back and regret that choice.

One guy I worked with for years, Mark, died of cancer. Not sure of his age, but early 60s I believe, so still *relatively* young (now that I'm in my 50s, the 60s don't seem as old as they used to). The morning before attending his funeral, standing at the kitchen counter making toast, it hit me – this guy that I knew and worked with for years will *never* get to make toast again. I don't know why this thought came to my head. I don't know why it was so profound for me at that moment. I don't know why it hit me so hard, but it did. For all I knew, maybe Mark didn't even like toast and would've never made it anyway, but just the fact that he *couldn't* make it ever again tore me up. Toast.

Mark worked as a Safety engineer on the F-15. He was friendly, thorough, detailed, and knowledgeable; and he maintained a veritable warehouse of past F-15 documentation in his mind and in his cubicle. If you had a question, any question, about the history of F-15 mishaps or incidents, or needed to know when a certain sentence in the Flight Manual changed, Mark was the guy to ask. If he didn't know the answer off the top of his head, in most cases he would find the answer for you, buried somewhere in the archives. Many times I stopped by his cube (he was just down the hall from me) and asked him some esoteric question, not entirely expecting an answer. If he didn't know the answer, I would say something like, "OK, no problem," and then shrug it off. (Note: In our line of work, there were many times when questions could simply not be answered.) Inevitably, later that day, here would come Mark visiting my cube, with some papers in hand documenting the very topic I was asking about. I had already shrugged it off. He certainly could've done the same, thus saving him time and effort, but he didn't. That was Mark.

Mark was also quiet, unassuming, and soft-spoken. I actually worked with Mark for many years before I learned of his pre-MDC career – he was an F-15 pilot in the Air Force. Well, blow me over with a feather! Mark had *none* of the traits that over the years I had learned to associate with pilots. If anybody had the ability to restore my faith in humanity (and pilots – ha!) it was Mark. It is a common expression used when somebody dies, and may sound trite, but Mark will be missed. Mark *is* being missed.

Throughout my 30+ years of work on the F-15, I participated in countless mishap investigations. The end result of several of those mishaps was that the pilot and/or WSO did not survive. None of these deaths were from combat. None. All were the result of accidents during training.

This makes the situations doubly sad, because in most cases, the mishap did not *have* to happen; it *could* have been avoided or prevented. The post-crash accident board would spend weeks looking at data, examining wreckage, and interviewing people in the hopes of reconstructing the mishap scenario to understand the underlying cause. In most scenarios, what we found was it was not some big event, but rather a culmination of small things that added up and caused the mishap. It's very likely if any one of those small things had not happened, the mishap would never have occurred.

Working all of those accident investigations made me appreciate the benefits of my career choice. When flying a high speed aircraft, especially in combat or training, things happen quickly. Pilots have precious little time to evaluate the situation and make decisions. Errors in judgment and/or faults with the aircraft can quickly lead to loss of control or collision. In stark contrast, I, as an engineer sitting at my desk, make an error in some analysis I'm working on, mistype a command, or just miss something I should've caught. Whatever the error was, in time, hopefully I discover it. I go back, correct my analysis, and then reformulate my conclusions, if that is even required. Entirely different scenario. I always get *tomorrow* to find and fix my mistakes, in an air-conditioned office with a comfy swivel chair and nobody trying to shoot at me, whether real or simulated.

I remember one vivid mishap where the pilot became disoriented while flying low to the ground at night in an unfamiliar area and ultimately hit a radio tower. I say *vivid* because miraculously, the Heads-Up Display (HUD) out-the-window video was pulled intact from the wreckage and we could view it. The amount of elapsed time between the pilot/WSO figuring out where the ground was to impact with the ground was only a few seconds – it all happened that fast. A few seconds. That is barely enough time for me, sitting at my computer in a comfy swivel chair, to type in a command and/or click the mouse. I make a mistake, I get tomorrow. These guys did not.

A typical mission for an F-15 is about 1-2 hours in length, if there is no aerial refueling. With refueling, missions can easily stretch to 3-4 hours, sometimes longer with multiple refuelings. Can you sit at a computer for 4 hours and not make a single mistake? Not mistype a command or misspell a word? Not click in the wrong window by accident? Not double-clicked where you should've only single-clicked? I certainly cannot. We make mistakes, simple mistakes, and we make them all the time. But we recover. We get tomorrow.

I give pilots and WSOs a lot of grief – that has been well established by now. But early on I said one of the words describing my relationship with them was *respect*. Amen. I have the utmost respect for the job they do and for the position they put themselves in on every mission. It's *their* butt in the seat if something goes wrong, not mine. It is *they* who have to make and react to split-second decisions, not me. I give them grief not out of malice. I give them grief (and get it back in return) because, for me, working in this industry without humor and banter would be borderline unbearable.

My last story is about Rick Husband. He was the commander of the ill-fated space shuttle Columbia STS-107. I knew Rick from his days as a USAF captain and F-15 test pilot at the CTF at Edwards AFB in the early 1990s. We did a lot of Performance & Flying Qualities testing on the F-15E, and he was one of our regular pilots.

I remember switching on the TV that day, February 1, 2003, and seeing the news coverage. My mind raced with thoughts of what the soon to be formed accident investigation board would do, how they would reconstruct the scenario, what they would find, and what they would likely never be able to know with any certainty. I knew, in the back of my mind, it would likely be something *small*. It's always the small things, hardly ever the big smoking gun. So, on that day, even though the accident was only minutes old, I *knew* months from now the accident board findings would say some little XYZ thing or action or procedure ultimately doomed Columbia and took Rick Husband and six others away from us. So sad. Such a loss. Such an unnecessary loss. Ditto for the space shuttle Challenger seventeen years earlier.

Rick Husband was a good guy, a pleasure to work with. He was a fun guy to have in the mission briefings and in the cockpit during mundane testing. He always had a good attitude. He was intelligent but humble. And if memory serves he always seemed to have a smile on his face. He was just a happy guy. And happiness was not a common trait in the CTF at that time, as there was tremendous pressure to get testing completed with limited resources so we could provide operational capability to the then new F-15E fleet.

I can still remember the day Rick got accepted to the incredibly selective astronaut program. He was walking around the CTF with the biggest grin on his face. He was on cloud nine, so happy, and we were all so happy for him, and so proud that one of our own had been selected to be an astronaut.

Space shuttle Columbia STS-107 mission patch. Courtesy of NASA.

Another appropriate quote from Mark Manson:

"Death scares us. And because it scares us, we avoid thinking about it, talking about it, sometimes even acknowledging it, even when it's happening to someone close to us... Yet, in a bizarre, backwards way, death is the light by which the shadow of all of life's meaning is measured. Without death, everything would feel inconsequential, all experience arbitrary, all metrics and values suddenly zero."

I'm not fixated on death or anything (yeah right, this coming from the guy who said he wasn't fixated on toilets, but then devoted multiple paragraphs to the discussion of toilets). Seriously though, I'm not at all overcome with the fear of death. I mean, I don't tempt it or anything – no walking up to the very edge of a cliff for me – but the thought of my eventual death doesn't consume me in any way. Plus, years ago I made a pact with God that he can't take me until I see the KC Chiefs win another Super Bowl. Dudes, I'm gonna live forever...

I'll end with another Mark Manson quote, "You too are going to die, and that's because you too were fortunate enough to have lived." Agree wholeheartedly.

CHAPTER 23
END OF A CAREER

"We, the unwilling, led by the unknowing, are doing the impossible for the ungrateful. We have done so much, for so long, with so little, we are now qualified to do anything with nothing."
  – Unknown

Many people have asked why I retired at a relatively young age (54). Lots of reasons for sure. Overall, work was a balance of the fun stuff to be enjoyed, compared to the bullshit that must be tolerated. After 33 years it just seemed to get to the point where the bullshit was overwhelming the fun.

Being a bunch of engineers who like all things numerically oriented, we came up with the term *Give-a-Shit* (GAS) factor to express our current mental state. In engineer speak, my GAS factor was at an all-time low.

↑ Ron   ↑ Leigh

...F-15SA FLIGHT TESTING KEEPS GETTING FURTHER AND FURTHER BEHIND.

Also, not too long before I left Boeing, the USAF decided to *retire* F-15E#1 to the desert boneyard at Davis Monthan AFB (see following photo). This is the jet I saw take off from St. Louis on its maiden flight in 1986. This is the jet I spent years at Edwards AFB monitoring data from. This is the jet, along with E#2, we used for wholesale updates to the aerodynamic database. Remembering watching E#1 take off from St. Louis on its *first* flight, then watching it take off on its *last* flight, and then seeing photos of it sitting shrink-wrapped in the desert... something just clicked within me. Was it a sign? Maybe it was time for me to give it up too?

Photo of F-15E#1 (tail number 86-0183) in the boneyard at Davis Monthan AFB, Arizona. Photo credit unknown.

And unbelievably, I ran out of staples. On my first day of work, way back in 1984, a fellow engineer showed me to the stationery supplies window, a *kid in the candy store* kind of wonderland where one could stock up on all those items that an engineer would find necessary in the daily execution of his or her duties. Pencils, pens, markers, pads of quad paper, boxes of graph paper, notebooks, binders, scissors, paper clips, etc. – almost more than one could carry. One of those necessary items was the ubiquitous black Bostitch B8 stapler, complete with a red box of 5,000 staples. I joked with my fellow engineer that if I ever ran out of staples, it might be time to retire. Crap. It happened. Apparently, I had used my rugged Bostitch stapler 5,000 times (without fail I might add). If there ever was going to be a sign, that was it. It was time to go.

As a parting gesture, the final words on my white board are shown in the following photo. There was also something about a parting email, but I won't go into that here.

"TAKE CARE OF YOUR FRIENDS, BECAUSE THERE
WILL COME A TIME WHEN YOU'RE NOT MUCH FUN TO
BE WITH AND THERE IS NO REASON TO LIKE YOU
EXCEPT OUT OF LONG-STANDING HABIT."

GARRISON KEILLOR

"I THINK MY TIME HAS COME."

RON PHILLIPS

To be honest, I'm not really sure how to end this book. It seems like I've spent a lifetime dishing out crap to pilots, and getting it back in spades. It's been mostly fun. If it weren't fun, I wouldn't have dragged my butt out of bed and gone to work each day for 33 years. And as much as I like to highlight the differences between us, most engineers and pilots in this industry have the same goal – to make their aircraft the best it can be at whatever it does. So, at least in that regard, one could lump engineers and pilots together – we're both necessary evils, I suppose.

End of a Career

How about I finish the book with another quote...

"The ultimate responsibility of the pilot is to fulfill the dreams of the countless millions of earthbound ancestors who could only stare skyward... and wish." – Unknown

That sounds kind of touchy-feely, huh? And definitely out of character for me. So, I'll finish with this quote from comedian George Carlin instead...

"Some people see things that are and ask, Why?
Some people dream of things that never were and ask, Why not?
Some people have to go to work and don't have time for all of that."

Much better. And much closer to reality.

R2LB: The trouble with life is, you're halfway through it before you realize it's a do-it-yourself thing.

CHAPTER 24
ACKNOWLEDGEMENTS

I was trying to write my acknowledgements, but was having some difficulty. How many books does one read where the author has a seemingly endless list of people to acknowledge? I have a few to directly acknowledge, but no long list, so am I doing something wrong?

Typically authors put forth a list of people who helped them with their struggle to write the book – the late hours, the constant writing and rewriting, the rushed deadlines, etc. Really? I obviously did something wrong. Struggle? Not really. Late hours? Never. Deadlines? None. Retirement has its advantages...

So, the author then expresses appreciation for all the encouragement and moral support during the book writing process. Encouragement? Maybe some. Moral support? No. Well, at least a *partial* no. Most people, including my kids, didn't even know I was writing this book until the first draft was essentially finished. My wife, upon learning I was going to write a book about engineers and pilots, offered a heartfelt, "That's nice, honey."

[Author's note: When my wife uses the word *honey* in reference to me, it's a code word. In reality, *honey* loosely translates into "my stupid husband, whom I, for some reason, choose to love and tolerate in spite of his idiotic ways." The sad part is it took me almost twenty years of marriage to figure that out. But you should've been there that day when I *did* figure it out. Proverbial fly on the wall kind of stuff. In a conversation that fateful day she happened to roll her eyes and call me *honey*. I saw the eyes. It clicked. I put two and two together. My mind instantly raced back in time to all the previous times she had called me that, and it all became clear. Crystal. *Honey* was not just some routine pet name she used. She only used that word when, in her mind, I did or said something stupid. The gig was up. I confronted her. She couldn't deny it. Busted. From that day on, any time she called me *honey*, I would give her that look that says without words, "Really? You really think I'm *that* stupid?" Just to be clear, she still refers to me as *honey* on occasion. But at least now she has to *think* about it first, which has the beneficial effect that she typically only uses it when I say or do something that truly is stupid. In all fairness, my wife has a different recollection of how all of this transpired. But this is how I remembered it.]

OK, so the author then expresses gratitude and/or apologies to his family and friends and/or pets for putting up with them whilst being all-consumed in the book writing process. Me consumed? No. Put up with? No. I wrote this book in my basement office during the day while my wife was at work. My kids are essentially grown and gone. My pets are two cats who sleep 23 and a half hours a day regardless if I'm writing or not. What I'm telling you is I initially wrote this book with little to no direct help from, nor any inconvenience to, any person or animal. No living creature was harmed during the writing of this book, as it were. Well, I take that back. I did go deer hunting last fall. But I did not include any deer hunting stories, so my previous statement stands.

I may have one exception to that *inconvenience* part. Cats #1 and #2 would routinely alternate sitting on my lap while I was at my desk typing. One day, however, Cat #1 did the unthinkable, the unforgiveable. She hopped up *on* my desk, and proceeded to saunter across my keyboard, inserting string after string of characters (luckily she didn't step on the *backspace* key). "No! I'm writing a book!" Cat #1, not being much for verbal commands, stood firm. So, admittedly, there might've been a slight *push* involved in removing her carcass from my keyboard. So sorry. She landed on her feet (it's what cats do), and gave me a long, pathetic "*meow*," which loosely translated to, "Writing a book, huh? That's nice, honey."

So, up until completion of the first draft, the writing of the book was never really an imposition on any *person* other than myself. But then came the review process.

The first draft would be reviewed by my three kids and a test pilot buddy. And in this context, *buddy* means a person with whom I spent years giving grief to, but who nonetheless opted to remain on cordial speaking terms with me. Thank you for that.

The test pilot buddy review was actually pretty benign, consisting of the expected grammar and punctuation errors noted, along with some technical content corrected. Minor stuff in the grand scheme of things.

Then came the editing comments from my kids. Prior to reading the first draft the overall feeling was, "Oh cool, Dad wrote a book." After reading the first draft it became, "Oh no, Dad wrote a book." Terrible punctuation. Terrible grammar. Terrible usage. Questionable writing style. Dubious content. Too opinionated. Too one-sided. Too brutal. I specifically asked for honesty from them. I got it. Don't hold back just because I'm your father. They did not. *Conceited ass with a big watch* seemed to be the consensus.

Devastated. Thoughts of giving up on the book project altogether were seriously entertained. But then test pilot buddy talked me off the ledge.

Two things had to be done...

First, most of the *terrible* punctuation, grammar, and usage were fixed. I am an engineer, not an English literature or poetry major. Reading and writing were things that *had* to be done to pass courses, they were neither things I *wanted* to do nor exceled at. This is the only time one will hear an apology from me for my education choice. I'm sorry.

Second, my kids had to be convinced that *conversational style* was a real thing, and writing a book such as this in that style was indeed acceptable. A struggle? Yes. Accomplished? A bit grudgingly perhaps, but yes. You may remember the mentioning of my kids as being very well read. Oh yeah. Tons of books consumed. All the great classics. All the great authors. This first draft they held in their hands was not a classic, nor was it ever destined to be. Their father is not a great author, nor is he ever destined to be. Once they came to grips with those two concepts, they warmed considerably. Or settled, perhaps? Either way, I truly thank each of my kids for caring enough to rip me to pieces, and then put me back together. Humpty Dumpty as it were.

Given having *both* parents being engineers, and all three kids choosing educations and careers having *nothing* to do with engineering, I should be thankful they did opt to put me back together, I suppose.

You may recall I said *most* of the punctuation, grammar, and usage issues were fixed. That is because *conversational style* allows the author to take some liberties with strict usage rules in order to let the content flow more like a true face-to-face conversation. Whew. Whoever invented that style must've been thinking about engineers. So, whoever you are, thank you. Thank you from the bottom of my functioning illiterate heart.

My wife did a thorough review after the first draft corrections were made. She found another dozen or so errors. Huh? How was that possible? I had written, re-written, read, and re-read those words a hundred times by then – how could there still be errors? Ahh, the mind reads what it *wants* to read, not necessarily the actual words in print. I knew that was a *thing*, but now it hit much closer to home. It amazed me how many times I could read right through improper words and not catch them. Thanks, honey. I needed that.

I need to acknowledge Scott Adams – the creator of the Dilbert cartoon. I'm no doubt not the only engineer to say this, but did he sit in the cubicle next to me for 33+ years, or what? So, so many Dilbert cartoons were incredibly spot on, as were hundreds of other cartoons with just a simple tweak of a word or two, or adding a coworker's name to a character. Dilbert cartoons were a perfect daily snapshot of my work experience. Amazing... Or sad... Or maybe both.

I used quite a few pilot and engineer jokes, and most have been around for years and years. I honestly have no idea who to acknowledge for them. I, for certain, did not write any of them myself. So, thanks to whoever was witty enough to come up with them on their own.

I would like to thank Willy Peeters for the cover cartoon. He dedicated his time and effort to take an already great F-15 cartoon and modify it to emulate F-15E#1 in order to more closely fit the topics of this book. Thank you for that.

It's an odd twist of fate that, quite possibly, the person who deserves the *most* acknowledgement is a WSO – Junkman. He convinced me to write this book in the first place. He kept urging me to write, and I kept dismissing him, arguing I didn't think the topic was book-worthy. He won. I lost. Thanks Junkman.

Acknowledgements

One obvious acknowledgement must go to my dad. He never had a call sign. Or if he did, he never told us what it was (I don't remember ever seeing that grimaced look, so I assume he was telling us the truth). I'm not entirely sure, but I don't think call signs were an integral part of fighter pilot lore back in the 1960s. But like I mentioned earlier, if my dad had not chosen to be a fighter pilot, my career may have taken a very different path. I like to think he chose wisely. For certain I chose wisely – no regrets from me.

Along with my dad, the following aircrew should be recognized (in no particular order that you know of). Many of these pilots and WSOs unknowingly contributed significantly to this book simply by being themselves. To be fair, not all of these people were stereotypical pilots or WSOs – hey, some were actually decent human beings – ha! Buy me a beer and I'll tell you which is which. Again, call signs only. Note there were also a few test pilots I've worked with who did not have, or chose not to use, a call sign. In these instances, I took the liberty of making up call signs for them. Sorry dudes.

Flood	Dragon	Junkman	Snidely	Bull
Spoons	Peedawg	Snitch	Phat	Mad
Hurled	Professor	GeeJay	Fletch	Fangs
Star	Nomas	Swoop	Bluce	Rabbit
Pokey	Iceman	Herc	Moose	Boxman
Dudley	Hollywood	Ritalin	Gus	Stump
Beast	Tonka	Sparrow	Sled	Hyde
MOS	Razor	Junior	Smurf	Laz
File	O.P.	Chopper	Surf	Fuze
Killbird	Brewdog	Cologne	Preacher Bob "PB"	

I should offer some special acknowledgement to the pilots/WSOs who provided me with most of my humorous material – Flood, Dragon, Bull, Spoons, Junkman, Snidely, and Peedawg. You know, maybe do something nice for them? Say, give them a complimentary signed copy of my book? Hmm. OK, I gave it some thought. Nah.

I should also acknowledge many of the hundreds of engineers I've worked with over the years. In keeping with my policy of not using full names, it seems like an extended list of first names would be relatively boring and meaningless, so I'll dispense with that. It's worth noting that a few engineers actually had call signs or nicknames. Really? Engineers with call signs? Yeah, I don't understand it either, but I don't write the rules. If you want to repeat, "Engineers with call signs – aww how cute is that?" I wouldn't argue with you. My nickname, you ask? Buy me that beer and we'll talk...

I could also acknowledge many of the managers I've had to deal with over the years. On second thought, that's probably an entirely new and different book. In lieu of that, how about this...

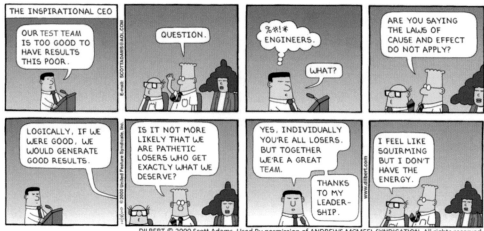

DILBERT © 2000 Scott Adams. Used By permission of ANDREWS MCMEEL SYNDICATION. All rights reserved. The cartoon text has been modified with permission for this book only.

I would like to acknowledge one person by full name, Jack Abercrombie. Jack was the head of the Aerodynamics Department at McDonnell Aircraft when I started working there. In fact, it was Jack who interviewed and hired me. That hiring process was a bit funny as well, like so many other things in my career.

So, indulge me one last time, the last, very last I promise, side story...

I was in my final co-op assignment, the summer before my senior year in college, working with the F-15 aerodynamics group – a group, unbeknownst to me at the time, destined to be my home for the vast majority of my career. Jack's secretary called and informed me that he would like to arrange a time for my interview for a full-time position. Wow, I had never spoken to a department head's secretary before. A suitable time was arranged, and by *suitable* I mean any damn time Jack wanted. Co-op students did not *dictate* schedule to department heads.

I was a bit nervous, to say the least. Jack, ahem *Mister* Abercrombie, was seven steps above me in the engineering food chain, although one could argue that co-op students weren't regular employees, thus didn't even occupy a step. Regardless of how one wanted to count it, a co-op student was the *lowest* position on the engineering staff, and the department head was the *highest*. Yes, I was nervous.

The interview day arrived and the funny, or odd, started. *Jack came to me.* We worked in separate buildings and I fully expected to hop on a company van and make the trip over to Building 33 for the interview. But no, Jack shows up early and strolls down the aisle, *my aisle*, in Building 1. Took me by surprise. In hindsight it shouldn't have been too much of a surprise, as this group was *his* group, these people were *his* people, and he was the department *head*. Jack needed neither an invitation nor permission to come talk to someone... anyone...

Jack walks up to my desk, stacked several feet deep in fan-fold computer printouts, and says, "Hi Ron, I'm Jack Abercrombie. I needed to be in Building 1 to talk with some folks anyway, so why don't we head to an empty conference room and knock this thing out?" Umm... Sure...

The *interview* lasted at most five minutes. It would've been only two minutes had we not exchanged a few requisite pleasantries. We sat down and he said, "Well, Ron, your group here has been pleased with your work so far. What will happen next is you should expect to get an offer in the mail within the next few months. And then you will have a few months to accept. Any questions? Good."

Remember all the self-help information about *how* to interview and *what to expect* during an interview? Remember memorizing and rehearsing lines for an interview? Remember Auntie Em telling you to be sure not to mumble, that you need to *annunciate*? (The importance of which was gleaned because of the fact it took her *four* seconds to say the word *annunciate*.) Remember trying to anticipate what questions you might be asked? Remember having the answer, in advance, to that most dreaded of all questions, "What would you say is your greatest weakness?" I do. I remember *all* of that. Yet I needed *none* of that. I'll bet Jack found great amusement knowing that, during the days between his secretary's call and the actual interview, I was busy tormenting myself. (In hindsight I'll bet he never gave me a passing thought. Ron who?)

Years prior to his role as department head of Aerodynamics, Jack was THE aerodynamics guy on the F-15. That was before my time at McDonnell, so I never had the opportunity to work directly with or learn directly from him, but his name was known to all. Whenever I heard the phrase "standing on the shoulders of giants" I thought of Jack. You could not pick up a historical F-15 document or report without seeing his name on it, or seeing his influence in it. In football speak, it would be akin to writing the history of the American Football League and not mentioning *Lamar Hunt* (sorry... my KC heritage showing through).

In several ways, Jack and I had similar careers. Jack did a lot of wind tunnel testing. Jack did multiple extended tours at Edwards AFB monitoring the original F-15A/B flight testing. He lived in the desert. He had a dirt bike. He wrote about his life and work in the desert (as yet unpublished memoir). And he *loved* the F-15. As department head, Jack had to represent every aircraft program McDonnell was working on, but you knew where his heart laid. Of that there was no doubt.

Jack was tall, dark, and handsome, and as rumor had it, very popular among the ladies. He also rose to the level of department head. These were where the similarities came to a halt, rather abruptly I might add.

So, I thank Jack for hiring me. I thank him for *being* the F-15, for putting that airframe in such a good position in terms of capability and performance that derivatives of it are still being rolled off the assembly line today – *fifty* years later, with no end in sight. I thank him for being those proverbial shoulders we could stand on. When I was a young engineer, I secretly hoped to work on the F-15 for my entire career, but never imagined it would be an actual possibility – because aircraft programs just didn't last that long. I knew I would have to move on to something else one day. One day never came. In fact, the F-15 program outlasted me.

During the F-15SA development, we had many technical information exchange meetings, and would invite several of the retired *greybeards* to get their insight and perspective on what we were adding or changing. During the start of one such meeting, we went around the conference room doing self-introductions and got to Jack. He mentioned his background and all the aircraft he had worked on, but then added, "The F-15 is *my baby*." The introductions continued around the room and then came to me. I stated the requisite bio information, but then added, "Yes, the F-15 is without a doubt Jack's baby, but I've been making the *child support payments* for the past twenty years."

Neither Jack nor I, during that brief five minute interview so long ago, would've ever dreamed that we'd be sitting across from each other, 35 years later, discussing how to make the F-15 *even better*. What a ride.

Photo of the author at Nellis AFB, Las Vegas, Jan 2019. You may notice that Nellis is *home of the fighter pilot*, not *home of the engineer*. I don't think that's a coincidence.

ACRONYMS / ABBREVIATIONS / DEFINITIONS

Acronyms are just one of those necessary evils within the Aerospace industry. You may hate them, but you can't live without them. So, for clarity sake, here's a list I have used in this book.

ABS — Antilock Braking System. A system that, apparently, needs to be tested on every car you rent? Preferably with some unsuspecting person riding in the passenger seat.

AE — Aerospace Engineering. A college degree program. A profession.

AFB — Air Force Base. A place from which to conduct flights and play golf.

AFMC — Air Force Materiel Command. An organization with a nice patch.

AMRAAM — Advanced Medium Range Air-to-Air Missile. Service date 1991. It was *advanced* back then, not sure what it is now, but the name stuck.

AOA — Angle of Attack. The *angle* between the oncoming air or relative wind and a reference line on the airplane or wing. Yeah, don't worry about it, half of the pilots don't know either.

ATC — Air Traffic Control. Air traffic controllers are one step above pilots on the aviation food chain, at least in their minds.

CAS — Control Augmentation System. The automated part of the F-15 flight control system that attempts to make up for gross buffoonery on the part of the pilot.

CFD — Computational Fluid Dynamics. Computational smoke and mirrors. Don't believe a thing you see.

CMSU — Central Missouri State University. A liberal arts college just south of Kansas City. No engineers.

CPA — Certified Public Accountant. Not an engineer.

CTF — Combined Test Force. A test team comprised of military personnel and contractors.

EE — Electrical Engineering. A degree program for people who either can't cut it as Aerospace engineers, or are trying to avoid working with pilots. The first is understandable. Ditto for the second.

EP — Emergency Procedures.

ER — Engineering Realization. A bit of wisdom picked up during the course of a career in engineering.

FAA — Federal Aviation Administration. ATCs work for the FAA, which reports to the DOT, which reports to the POTUS. I'm not defining the rest of those. Look them up if you're interested.

FMRC — Flight Manual Review Conference. A place for pilots to gab amongst one another and for engineers to waste valuable time.

GAS — Give-a-Shit. A factor used to quantify one's mental state of being.

GCWS — Ground Collision Warning System. A system designed by engineers that tries to save pilots from themselves.

GIB	Guy in Back.
GPA	Grade Point Average. That thing one needed to get a job in the Aerospace industry.
GPS	Global Positioning System. That thing that tells you when you're lost.
HUD	Heads-Up Display. A display of critical flight information projected in front of the pilot, so they don't have to spend much time looking down at instruments inside the cockpit.
IAS	IRST Adapter Shape.
ICMU	I Crack Myself Up. Yes, sometimes I do.
IM	Instant Message. That thing that allows you to get into trouble in an instant.
IRST	Infrared Search & Track.
KC	Kansas City. Home of the Chiefs. Home of the Royals (who beat the Cardinals in '85). Boyhood home of Ron Phillips.
KISS	Keep It Simple Stupid. Attributed to Kelly Johnson.
LA	Los Angeles.
LSD	Lysergic acid diethylamide. A hallucinogenic drug. Also known as acid. Effects typically include altered thoughts, feelings, and awareness of one's surroundings. Many users see or hear things that do not exist. Similar effects as being a gifted test pilot.
Mach	The ratio of a vehicle's speed relative to the speed of sound. The expression *Mach 2* would refer to flying at *twice* the speed of sound. Named for Ernst Waldfried Josef Mach, a German physicist and philosopher, who was a major influence on logical positivism and American pragmatism. Plus his name just sounds really cool. So cool, in fact, Gillette names a razor after him, *Mach 3*, even though razors have absolutely nothing to do with flying three times the speed of sound.
MoST	Missouri Institute of Science and Technology.
MSM	Missouri School of Mines. Even older name of MoST.
MDA	Minimum Design Altitude. The minimum altitude at which to always give a GCWS warning. Agreed to by all, or some, or few, or none...
MDC	McDonnell Douglas Corporation. Designer and builder of the mighty F-15 Eagle – the world's greatest fighter.
NAS	Naval Air Station. A place from which to conduct flights, but not play golf.
NASA	National Aeronautics and Space Administration. An independent agency of the USG responsible for the civilian space program, as well as aeronautics and aerospace research.
NSVMR	Not So Vague Movie Reference.
OMG	Oh My God. Valley girl speak.
OML	Outer Moldline. The part of the aircraft that feels the oncoming air.
PSWT	Polysonic Wind Tunnel.
RIO	Radar Intercept Officer. The Navy's official term for the GIB.
RSM	Random Stick Monkey. The pilot in the front seat. A term of endearment.

RTB	Return To Base. That thing aircrew do right before happy hour.
R2LB	Rule to Live By. A snippet containing an insightful life lesson.
6-DOF	Six Degrees of Freedom. An incredibly complex set of equations that only the most highly educated and highly motivated aerospace engineers could possibly comprehend.
SPO	System Program Office. USAF organization that oversees a weapons program.
SRB	Safety Review Board.
TIS	Test Information Sheet. A document engineers pour their very heart and soul into writing. Typically not read by pilots.
TPS	Test Pilot School. A place where regular pilots go to become *gifted*.
TRB	Technical Review Board.
TSM	Time Safety Margin. Don't ask.
TWA	Trans World Airlines. Kaput.
TWD	Test Working Document. The Navy's name for a TIS.
UMR	University of Missouri Rolla. Old name of MoST.
USAF	United States Air Force. The country club service.
USG	United States Government.
USN	United States Navy.
VMR	Vague Movie Reference. What engineers live for?
VCR	Vague Commercial Reference. A VMR for ads. You were thinking Video Cassette Recorder perhaps? Those are archaic. Get with the times.
WSO	Weapon System Operator. Also called the GIB. Sits behind the RSM.
WW2	World War 2. Please tell me I didn't have to define this?

Made in the USA
Columbia, SC
16 December 2019